Real Men Wear
Boxer Shorts

Qualities That Make Men Real

Dewey Friedel

Treasure House

An Imprint of
Destiny Image Publishers, Inc.®
P.O. Box 310
Shippensburg, PA 17257-0310

"For where your treasure is
there will your heart be also." Matthew 6:21

ISBN 1-56043-847-9

For Worldwide Distribution
Printed in the U.S.A.

Treasure House books are available through these fine distributors outside the United States:

Christian Growth, Inc.
Jalan Kilang-Timor, Singapore 0315

Vine Christian Centre
Mid Glamorgan, Wales, United Kingdom

Rhema Ministries Trading
Randburg, South Africa

Vision Resources
Ponsonby, Auckland, New Zealand

Salvation Book Centre
Petaling, Jaya, Malaysia

WA Buchanan Company
Geebung, Queensland, Australia

Successful Christian Living
Capetown, Rep. of South Africa

Word Alive
Niverville, Manitoba, Canada

Inside the U.S., call toll free to order:
1-800-722-6774

Dedication

With gratitude, I dedicate this book foremost to my high school sweetheart, friend, lover, and wife for 25 years, Ronda. Her life is the most wonderfully honest example of transparency and sincerity I have ever witnessed.

To our son Isaac who is a constant joy and challenge, and the greatest gift God has ever given us.

To George and Ida Mae Friedel whose caring hearts and sacrifices always created an atmosphere of trust and love. No man ever had greater parents.

To my sisters Diane and Carolyn who taught me so much about women and myself and who always loved me unconditionally.

To Ronda's parents Dick and Neta Goodell who always give us a place of rest and peace.

To my special buddies Randy Barr, Deo Miller, and Dr. Bill Peters for their sharing dreams with me.

To Michael Chitwood and John Avanzini for always being there when I've needed a strong arm.

To Oral Roberts who taught me 25 years ago how to trust God and walk in faith.

To my administrator Torleif Brattli who has shown me that Christians can be loyal and function with integrity.

To my secretaries, Sandy and Pat, for all their assistance.

To the real men who oversee the church: Dick, Jim, Bill, Doug, and Will; and all the marvelous people God has called to the family and vision of Shore Christian Center.

To our family away from home: Clayton and Frances Newman; Barbara Peters, Loretta and Marty Tencza, and Ina Corbo.

Finally, to the many scholars, leaders, and teachers who influenced my life in this area, and from whose works I gleaned much insight.

Contents

Foreword

I knew when I'd read just the Introduction and the first chapter of Pastor Dewey Friedel's manuscript, *Real Men Wear Boxer Shorts*, that the finished book would be the most unusual book I'd ever read. I was right. When I finished reading the manuscript, I said to myself, *Nobody reading this book will be able to lay it down!*

Who are you? You'll know when you finish reading this book.

How do you protect your manliness or your womanliness? You'll find the answers as never before from this book.

How do you become successful by being a God-directed human being? You'll get your answer in this book.

I love Dewey Friedel, a top graduate of Oral Roberts University and Princeton Theological Seminary; he's a "real man" who pastors an innovative and anointed church. Plus he is a man's man and a man whom godly women honor. I predict you'll "feel" changed in your total being, as I do, when you let the invigorating and captivating power of this book take hold of your life.

Oral Roberts

Introduction

What do "boxer shorts" have to do with being a "real man"? You'll have to read the first chapter to figure that one out, but it will make sense in the end. No, I don't own stock in "Fruit of the Loom," but I want my great-grandchildren to enjoy life in a safe world run by real men and women who know their God. That means that you and I need to get busy, because real men don't just grow in trees or public school systems like evolutionists would have us believe. They are mentored and trained to become men.

"Then the Lord God called to the man, and said to him, 'Where are you?' " (Gen. 3:9 NAS). When God called for Adam in the Garden of Eden, it wasn't because He didn't know where Adam was. He was asking Adam, "Where are you in relationship to Me? Are you going to take the mark of the beast, or are you going to walk clothed in My glory?"

"And he said, 'I heard the sound of Thee in the garden, and I was afraid because I was naked; so I hid myself' " (Gen. 3:10 NAS). How did Adam know he was naked? He had lost his covering, the glory of the Lord.

Once Adam and Eve chose to follow satan's advice, they turned from the legitimate path to God-likeness to walk in an illegitimate direction. The result was deadly. The two unique creatures created in God's own image and likeness, who had been clothed with His glory, now started to look like animals. God basically said, "I can't allow you to dress in fruit and fig leaves. There must be a blood sacrifice for this deed. You deserve to die yourselves, but I will provide a substitute for you." This led to Jesus Christ becoming the great substitutionary sacrifice for all of us.

The mark of the beast has been on our hands since the fall. We use our hands to hurt each other instead of embracing one another. Nebuchadnezzar became like a beast, even though he ruled most of the "civilized" world of that time. He stood at his balcony window declaring, "I am god," after falling into the same temptation that trapped Eve. As a result, God confronted Nebuchadnezzar and told him, "You must become a beast." So for seven years, Nebuchadnezzar grew long hair, and his nails became like birds' claws. He was like a werewolf; he was a beast of the field on all fours. Thank God for restoration. After seven years he came to his senses. He looked up and called on the Lord God. He submitted once again to God, and miraculously, the beast once again became a restored man.

Mankind has become animal-like. We have abused every gift God has given us. Our sexuality has become bestial, and we kill and fight one another. Perhaps it is made worse by the fact that in the past hundred years since the Industrial Revolution, men have become removed from their earthly fathers. For millennia fathers were very close to their sons. In some ways fathers were a type of food for their sons; they were together all the time. The son could almost taste his dad's sweat as he labored to train the son as an apprentice in his craft or trade—as heir of the family business. Fathers and sons remained very close in both work and play. Even the animals were caught up in this synergy of the closeness of life. When it got cold, often the dogs would come in and sleep with their owners; they needed the dogs' body heat. It's hard to do that with a computer or a drill press.

It has only been in the past few decades of this planet's history that we detoured from natural paternal relationship and became lost. We can create industrial and technological megaplexuses, but we don't know who we are as men anymore. Women have also suffered because they have been trodden under the heels of confused men ruling as beasts.

Statisticians tell us that fathers spend only about 10 minutes a day with their children, and most of that time is spent in such "meaningful" conversation as: "Did you pick up this? Did you clean your room? Did you wash your hands? Did you brush your teeth?" So much for "quality time" with our children. It wasn't always like that. But now our little boys grow up experiencing a separation from Dad, and it's very painful for both sides. All of us grow up with all kinds of images of what it is to be a man, and yet inside, we know that our images don't quite hit it.

Isn't it interesting that during the past hundred years we've experienced a *simultaneous* separation from both our earthly dads *and* our heavenly Father? In the past century, we have also lost our manhood.

Moms can't train us in manhood. They can teach us to be sensitive in relationships and how to understand feelings. They teach us about the earth and how we must respect our environment. However, moms don't teach us how to be warriors, and that is part of our manly nature.

You see, the warrior in you is the one who rises up when the other side of you is saying, "Okay, you've done enough right now. Quit and go get some ice cream. You deserve it." The warrior says, "Uh uh. You're not finished. It's not time for the ice cream." Most of us still need to be trained and initiated in what it means to be a warrior. The flip side is this: A warrior will become an abuser of womenfolk if the warrior doesn't have a king, and that's what we've faced in this generation.

You may be grieving because your dad has passed away and you were never properly bonded to him. One man whose father was living told me, "I really need help. My dad is not a Christian and I cannot relate to him. It's a deep grief for me."

I told him, "I want you to do something. I want you to go to your dad and have him say, 'I love you.' Then have him lay his hands on top of your head and say, 'God bless you.' "

He said, "Well, I don't think my dad will do it."

I told him to try it anyway, and for the first time in his life his dad ended up saying, "Son, I love you." And even though he was not a Christian he laid his hands on his son's head and said, "God bless you." That sealed something in this man; he came back all smiles because God had done something. There had been a bonding.

Some of us need to get away for a day or two with our dads if they're still alive. We need to say, "Dad, if it's got to be a fishing trip or whatever, we're going to get together." Look at your dad "eyeball to eyeball" and tell him, "I love you Dad, and I've missed you all of my life."

Every man needs a spiritual mentor. A select few find their spiritual mentor in their physical father, but the estrangement of the last century has made that sadly uncommon. No one can take my dad's place. He has been and remains the greatest Christian example in my life. Yet God also gave me an older man named Ern Baxter to become a spiritual mentor in my life. He passed away about two years ago, but nobody will ever take his place either. When I first met Ern, I knew we had something; there was a special chemistry between us. When I ministered in Canada some of the believers there said, "You're more like Ern Baxter than any man we've ever met. We watched you for a week, and you even have the same study styles! You go in your room, lock your door, and don't come out until four hours later. Then you take a quick break and immediately dive back into the Word."

It is obvious that my mentor made an impact on my life. Although Ern Baxter is gone, he continues to show up in me and in the lives of other men of God he influenced. He was more than a pastor to me; there was almost a father and son relationship between us. Every young man needs an older man who will carry him in his heart.

An Army sergeant can train you and teach you survival skills, but he can't really initiate you into full manhood because he doesn't carry you in his heart. However, when an older man of God prays, "Lord, show me some younger man that You want me to be attached to and train," then something powerful will happen. Paul saw the pattern when he instructed Titus, the "son" he had mentored, to have the older women teach the younger women to love their husbands and to exhort the younger men to live godly lives (see Titus 2:3-8). We all need an older man in the Lord who will carry us in his heart and say, "I really love you, and I delight in your obedience to the faith." There is healing in that, as well as godly training.

God wants to heal us and remove the mark of the beast so we can go on into wholeness. We must destroy the mark of the beast that has come against restored womanhood and restored manhood in the Lord Jesus Christ. We are called to live in the restored covenant, not in the past patterns of bestiality. We've been given "new clothes" in the Lord.

God hasn't called me to change you. No human being can change another human being. He has called me to inspire you to get as close to Jesus as possible so you will become like Him in a legitimate sense and walk in the image of God.

Dewey Friedel
July 1, 1995

Chapter 1

Mirror Man and White Underwear

"Come, see a man." One Sunday morning I quoted this brief four-word phrase of Scripture and told my congregation that if we advertised it in the newspaper, a massive crowd of women would probably come just to see if it were true!

> *And upon this came His disciples, and marvelled that He talked with the woman: yet no man said, What seekest Thou? or, Why talkest Thou with her? The woman then left her waterpot, and went her way into the city, and saith to the men, Come, see a man, which told me all things that ever I did: is not this the Christ?* (John 4:27-29)

I was only joking about the advertisement, but there is a serious side to this situation. We're facing a real shortage of manhood today! Our scarce supply of this supernatural resource has affected every aspect of our lives—including our government structures, our marriages and families, our churches, and our schools. We should have known that once the vital nutrient of manhood was subtracted from the diets of our children and institutions that anemia, sickness, and disease would surely follow. Today, our "liberated" nation is entering the twenty-first century with a possibly terminal case of masculine anemia!

The disciples of Jesus couldn't believe their Teacher was talking to a Samaritan "dog" woman in public. According to Levitical law she was unclean. Men just didn't speak with women like that in those days. Praise God, Jesus wasn't like other men! He challenged every archaic custom that was crafted to limit or control the plan of God. Jesus defied tradition to openly demonstrate in word and deed that women are of equal worth as men. This woman left that well carrying more than water in a jar. She became a carrier of the water of life by declaring to the leaders in her hometown, "Come, see a man!"

God wants people to see Christ in this generation of men! If they do, then everywhere we will hear them proclaim to their cities, "Come, see a man. I've found a *real man*. He's just like Jesus!" Our sick world longs to see the beautiful sight of real men who dare to walk in the purposes of God day in and day out!

It's a terrible thing to see a man in tattered clothing staggering down a littered city street, begging for pocket change with the smell of stale liquor on his breath. Most of us find ourselves somewhere between this picture of failure and degradation and Christ's picture of obedience to the will of God. There are eight types of men, and we desperately need deliverance from six of them! We have all been afflicted by the six sinful types in one way or another. Their infirmity holds us back from our manhood!

The Mama's Boy

You never really know whether this first brand of man is more in love with his wife or his mama. God wants us to love both, but He clearly expects us to cut the umbilical cord at some point! It is difficult to fulfill the purposes of God in manhood when you're still clutching to your mama's apron strings.

Micah perfectly matched the description of "Mama's boy" (see Judg. 17). Evidently he had been spoiled rotten as a boy because he still thought he could get away with robbery. When he secretly stole some of his mother's silver, she reacted in a wonderfully godly way by putting a curse on whoever stole her silver. Then Junior got scared. Finally he confessed to Mama that he had stolen her silver. Since she had always made Micah "number one" in her life, she told him, "Honey, you're forgiven. In fact, I think I'll give you some of this silver. Now, I want you to make molten images out of this silver, and I want you to be your own priest over the gods you make!" Micah liked that so much that he went one step further. He also hired himself a priest from the tribe of Levi so he could really set up his own religion the way he liked it.

Micah's mama should have taught her son responsibility. Instead, she supported his irresponsibilities and ensured that he would always remain a child. He thought society—or mama—owed him something. He set up his own self-centered universe, and faithfully attended his own church, which was devoted to the most important being in his world—himself.

The "Crybaby, Chicken Little" Man

This man always wants somebody else to do the job for him. If there is a conflict, he sends Mama to the door to take care of it. If the sky is falling, he cries about it until *somebody else* solves the problem. God made men to be protectors, but this kind of man is so fearful of others that he sends his wife or his mama out in front when trouble comes around!

Ahab, the wimpy husband of the wicked Jezebel, is the prize-winning "Chicken Little" of the Bible. He always allowed Jezebel to do whatever she wanted. One day, Ahab came home sucking his thumb (in First Kings 21:4 the Bible describes him as "heavy and displeased") because Naboth wouldn't sell him the vineyard he'd inherited from his father. This "great king of Israel" crawled into bed, pulled the sheets over his head, and whined until Jezebel came to his rescue. Jezebel, the schemer, organized a feast and invited Naboth to sit at the head table. She then planted two liars in the crowd who accused Naboth of something nasty, and he was stoned to death! "Chicken Littles" constantly complain about their problems, leaving the difficult situations to others. Real men deal with problems themselves. They don't leave it all to Mama.

The Mirror Man

This fine specimen of modern "manhood" takes an hour and a half in front of a mirror simply to fluff his hair with a hair dryer. The "unisex" idea spawned in the silly 1960's now dominates many areas of our society. The Mirror Man equates manhood with everything that is on the outside. (It's getting tough too because men and women are dressing more and more alike!) About a decade ago, men's underwear started looking just like women's panties, thanks in part to effeminate males who basically dominate the clothing design industry. Now, when you wake up in the morning, you can grab her underwear or yours because they both look alike! Both of them are silky and flimsy and...

Wait a minute! I may sound like a sexist, but I think *real men wear boxer shorts*! Whatever happened to the no-frills white underwear men used to wear? (When I preached this to my congregation, I threatened to have the ushers check out all the men of the church in my office, but then I came to my senses.)

The Mirror Man takes great pride in his outward appearance and in the opinions of others. Saul was brought low by this kind of thing. One day, he had just finished fluffing his hair in the mirror and was thinking, *My, what a handsome fellow I am!* Then he heard women in the streets singing, "Saul has killed his thousands...." He thought, *This is great. Women really love me!* Everything was fine until he heard them sing the second half of the stanza, "...but David has killed his ten thousands!" (see 1 Sam. 18:7) Saul was crushed because his self-image and his manhood were based on what people said about him instead of what God said about him.

The "Macho Lover" Man

This man is an undisciplined user. He uses women for his own selfish pleasure. Our society is riddled with this deadly image of manhood. Our music glorifies musicians and movie stars who casually have sex with countless women during their travels, while ignoring the sad reality that hundreds of lives, marriages, and childhoods were forever damaged or destroyed by their indiscriminate lust. The "Macho Lover" is insensitive to the things of God and he's insensitive to women.

Samson epitomizes this type of undisciplined man. How many times have you heard of men who were mightily used by God, but fell because of secret sexual sins? The church at Corinth often received powerful ministry from gifted people who were also deeply involved in sin (until the apostle Paul heard about it).

God wants us all to live holy lives, but His gifts aren't given because we are particularly holy. Whenever we slip out of the anointing and into our own flesh, we will always do the will of the flesh instead of the will of God. We all need brothers who will help us discipline ourselves. One thing is sure: Every Macho Man will meet his Delilah someday if he doesn't repent! God wants most of us to dwell securely for life with one marriage partner. (Only a few have the gift of celibacy.) Husbands, love your wives! That is where the fulfillment is! There is no hangover there, and there are no AIDS, or gonorrhea, or syphilis, or herpes! You won't be waking up in the morning and saying, "Oh my God. Why did I do that last night?!"

Mister Insensitive

This man chugs his beer and watches the Giants (or he gulps his Snapple Iced Tea and watches the Mets) while his wife across the room is dying from neglect. His wife needs to talk, but he is insensitive to her needs. Mighty man of God, how well do you relate to your wife when she faces pregnancy, menstrual cramps, and menopause (or the identity crisis brought on by her insensitive husband)? I'm sure you do the right thing. In fact, I'm sure that you would haul your carcass away from the game at the top of the fourth quarter and say (without growling), "Honey, I want you to get dressed up. I'm taking you out for dinner tonight—without the kids. I think you need to talk, and I need to listen; but we're going to do it in style!"

"Mr. Insensitive" constantly hunts for "something better," even at the expense of the most important things in his life! For only $2,000 more a year, he will pluck his family out of their stable surroundings and out of a good church. He'll jerk his wife away from all of her relationships, and pull the kids out of school without a thought—probably without even considering the fact that it will cost him $4,000 just to move! (There are some exceptions, of course. Sometimes you do have to move—just be sensitive to the needs of your spouse and children too.)

Mr. Right Reverend Billy Bob "Get It All Now!" Preacher Man

This is your dynamic, charismatic leader generally, and church leader especially. He says, "I want it now! I don't care about the future generation. I want it now—at any cost!" God wants us to touch the generations beyond our own. He wants to do something that lasts, and He wants to do it through us in our lifetime. That takes patience and long-term thinking. That also leaves out *Mr. Right Reverend Billy Bob "Get It All Now!" Preacher Man.*

The Normal Man

The "Normal Man" is a man who lives according to the biblical pattern recorded in Acts 13:22, which says, "And when He had removed him [Saul], He raised up unto them David to be their king; to whom also He gave testimony, and said, I have found David the son of Jesse, a man after Mine own heart, which shall fulfil all My will."

Now David is a man we can identify with. He was "Joe Average" on the outside, but he was special on the inside because he loved God and leaned on Him for everything. He absolutely failed morally when he committed adultery and arranged the cold-blooded murder of a woman's husband. God despised David's sin, and when He confronted him with it, David didn't make excuses. He deeply and genuinely repented of his sins (see his pattern for true repentance in Psalm 51). David couldn't bear to be separated from his God, and God blessed him for his pure heart, although his moral sin and murder cost him a son. God wants normal men, men who will draw close to Him with broken and contrite hearts to have their imperfections covered by His perfection.

The Perfect Man, Jesus

Jesus Christ went beyond the "normal man." He was the "perfect man." He was perfect in His emotions, His courage, His compassion, and His daily walk. He attracted thousands of women because He was a real man who treated women with gentleness—even when it wasn't the popular thing to do. He didn't look at women as sources of ego satisfaction, and He didn't try to control them.

Jesus was a *lion* from the tribe of Judah (the tribe of *loud, shouting*). He was a warrior! Every man has a warrior within, and whenever we try to deny it, we emasculate ourselves. (This has happened in our culture.) Many men in the Church today almost seem to be "neutered." They've lost their masculinity somewhere. They no longer seem to have the God-given instinct and power to protect and preserve.

The ultimate Man, Jesus Christ, is seeking men. True manhood seeks out men. The world fears the man who is secure in his manhood because he cannot be manipulated. Jesus couldn't even be frightened with death! Real manhood is the power to change and to create a new environment. We need to rediscover the manhood of Jesus and the "lion" side of His masculinity. He was a culture changer and a transformer of men and women. Now He is calling us to take that dominion mandate to our generation!

The problem is that when we come face to face with Jesus, we discover that our own brand of masculinity is nothing compared to His absolute power. Thus we run from the lion, and from true spirituality. Listen brother, it takes a real man to surrender to the truth about masculinity (just as it takes a real woman to admit and accept God's truth about true femininity). God wants to transform every man from a destroyer into a creator! He wants us to display manly strength and firmness, the kind that only comes from the Lion of Judah Himself! That brand of manhood displays toughness in the face of opposition. It demonstrates decisiveness in the face of uncertainty. It embodies protecting power in the face of danger. If Jesus Christ is in us, then we have a job to do in this life, and nothing can stop us until God's will is accomplished in our lives!

We need masculine warriors today! Our culture believes that the mark of true manhood is to reject Dad at the earliest age possible, but God wants to raise up authentic men who will run to face every challenge in the strength and anointing of the Lion of Judah!

Chapter 2

Jezebel Wants a Date

Now that you've stocked up on a manly brand of boxer shorts, I think you should know that somebody has her eyes on you. She dresses boldly with flamboyant style and eye-catching makeup, and she knows how to make a man look twice. Her name is Jezebel, and she wants to "take you out."

By the way, you're not the first man of God she's wanted to take out. Jezebel did everything she could to take out Elijah:

And Ahab told Jezebel all that Elijah had done, and withal how he had slain all the prophets with the sword. Then Jezebel sent a messenger unto Elijah, saying, So let the gods do to me, and more also, if I make not thy life as the life of one of them by to-morrow about this time. And when he saw that, he arose, and went for his life, and came to Beersheba... (1 Kings 19:1-3).

How could a "storybook woman" from the Old Testament be after you today? The answer may shock you. This woman "ain't no lady"! Jezebel is a spirit that is neither female nor male. Yes, the Jezebel in First Kings was a real person. She was a Phoenician princess who was married to Ahab, the king of Israel. Although Jezebel is probably the most wicked woman in the Old Testament, the real power behind her wickedness was an ancient spirit that also surfaces in the Book of Revelation thousands of years later. That same spirit is working around the clock right now to destroy the Church—and you.

This Jezebel spirit is neither masculine nor feminine, but it usually works through the unique charms of women because they tend to catch more men than other enticements. Jesus warned the Church of Thyatira about this malignant spirit in the Book of Revelation:

> *Notwithstanding I have a few things against thee, because thou sufferest that woman Jezebel, which calleth herself a prophetess, to teach and to seduce My servants to commit fornication, and to eat things sacrificed unto idols* (Revelation 2:20).

Jezebel's name means "without cohabitation." She refuses to live together with anybody in harmony—she always wants to control and dominate. The Jezebel spirit isn't any ordinary evil spirit; it is probably one of the dark "principalities" described by the apostle Paul:

> *For we wrestle not against flesh and blood, but against principalities, against powers, against the rulers of the darkness of this world, against spiritual wickedness in high places* (Ephesians 6:12).

The first Jezebel dominated and controlled her husband, King Ahab, and through him she brought all Israel under her control. She ordered the slaughter of the prophets of God and banned the worship of Jehovah. Her spineless husband abandoned God and erected shrines to

Baal, and she built groves devoted to the worship of the "female" deities of the Asherim. Both of these involved fertility worship through sexual deviation and the sacrifice of children.

During Jezebel's reign of terror with Ahab, only Elijah, 100 prophets hidden in a cave by Obadiah, and 7,000 followers of Jehovah managed to survive her devil-inspired purge of everything that had to do with the one true God.

Jezebel Thinks Big

The Jezebel spirit is never content with small winnings; it hungers for entire churches, nations, and kingdoms! It will patiently hammer at individual leaders and believers, but only if their fall will help bring down something really big (and preferably dear to God). The spirit of Jezebel is driven to destroy and profane the Kingdom of God, disrupt His order, and plant discord among the brethren.

The first thing Jezebel targets are male leaders such as pastors, presidents, and kings of nations. Well-known ministers, televangelists, and other leaders have fallen in the last two decades as never before, and more are to come. The body count has been even worse on the local front where many church pastors have fallen into sin and out of the ministry. What is happening? Jezebel is loose in the Church and God's people aren't doing anything about it!

Jezebel Loves Her Job

The "woman" who wants you really likes her job. Jezebel is a professional escort, and she's been at her job for thousands of years. She'll go everywhere you go and compromise everything that is dear to you. I think she has a whole trophy room filled with dirty boxer shorts marking the demise of countless mighty men who have fallen prey to her seductive ways. The Bible says, "Lest Satan should get an advantage of us: for we are not ignorant of his devices" (2 Cor. 2:11). The spirit of Jezebel uses six common devices or "believer deceivers" to seduce and reduce God's people.

    1. *There is a Jezebel in the flesh prepared for pastors and church leaders.*

One of the time-honored ways to win a battle quickly is to capture the king or leader of the opposing forces. The devil isn't an original thinker and neither is his "girlfriend." Jezebel targets the top man in every godly church organization. This evil spirit often sends along an attractive, gifted, and "understanding" young woman who has yielded to its lustful urgings, as Jezebel did. They unknowingly (or in some cases, purposely) seduce God's men and compromise their witness and leadership ability.

Men in leadership must constantly exercise special caution and wisdom to avoid falling into sexual sin because their spiritual position and authority can make them "attractive." Ern Baxter once said, "The Spirit of God makes anointed men attractive—even the ugly ones."

I have a firm policy of *never* counseling or meeting females alone. I always insist that another man of God, or my wife, be present with me before I will meet with a member of the opposite sex. If these conditions cannot be met, then I refuse to meet under such potentially dangerous circumstances. The apostle Paul didn't say we were to fight youthful lusts—he said we should flee them! (See Second Timothy 2:22.)

    2. *Jezebels are raised up or planted in local churches to infiltrate leadership, to steal the hearts of the sheep, and to lead unwary intercessors into rebellion.*

When the shepherd refuses to fall into Jezebel's arms, it often gets angry and goes to "Plan B." The "B" stands for "buck, blaspheme, belittle, and badger." Although spiritual gifts may operate through any believer, male or female, biblical church leadership has been placed on male shoulders. When church splits come, it is generally fueled by the jealousy and envy of somebody who secretly desires the top seat of power and honor. The Jezebel spirit just attaches itself to that desire.

The Jezebel spirit usually begins operating through a very spiritual woman in the church, and it will want to rob the church of the gift within that woman. Before you know it, there is disharmony in the home and discord is planted in the church. The root of bitterness spreads very quickly to other like-minded individuals, while the wimpish Ahabs in the church sit back and let it happen.

According to First Samuel 15:23, "Rebellion is as the sin of witchcraft." When we rebel against God's plan—whether His order happens to be politically correct that week or not—we are inviting in alien spirits from satan's realm. Jezebel has her makeup on and she is hunting for a house to live in.

Gifted female intercessors are some of Jezebel's favorite targets because they generally possess exceptional spiritual gifts and insights. At times, they may become frustrated with the "stupid pastor" who just can't seem to grasp the importance of the revelation they have received directly from God's throne. Once they despise God's "set man" and belittle or slander the undershepherd, they have set themselves in opposition to God and in alliance with Jezebel. That's a hard statement, but it is true.

3. *Victims—regardless of their calling or station in life—are initiated into sin to separate them from God's fellowship and the safety of His flock for easy destruction in isolation.*

The Mafia hasn't invented anything new. Satan and Jezebel have practiced the art of "implication" since the coup in the garden. The first thing Jezebel tries to do to any of us is to get us to sin. Whether the sin is big or small, whether it is an illicit affair or five minutes of a sensual movie after midnight in the privacy of your den, Jezebel knows when the bait has been taken. She is out to set the hook in your jaw! Once you have sinned, guilt sets in and your communication with God and the brethren is hindered or severed completely.

4. *Jezebel confuses and distorts family roles on a global scale and perpetuates her curses through the generations of wounded children.*

The family is a primary target of Jezebel's aggressive warfare. This spirit's all-out assault on the bedrock of marriage, fidelity, fatherhood, and motherhood undermines the health of the nations and tomorrow's generation. Jezebel wants to rip the security of covenant relationships right out of our hearts so rebellion and instability can take its place.

American society reflects the modern mirror image of Ahab's backwards household, where Jezebel ruthlessly called the shots while the emasculated king, "Chicken Little" Ahab, wimpered from his bed. Today, wimpish men sit at home while their wives function in critical spiritual spheres of church-related matters without the proper covering from their husbands. No wonder the modern woman is stereotyped as being hard, brazen, and independent! Is there no remedy for this twisted sister?

God created male and female *equal in value* but *different in function*. Man is the head, but he is to rule his household as Christ rules the Church—in *sacrificial love*, and in total dependence on God the Father. The issue is male leadership, not male dominance. It is concerned with womanhood *expressed*, not womanhood *suppressed*.

Isaiah 3:12 gives us a picture of the judgment on this country: "As for My people, children are their oppressors, and women rule over them...." This is modern America under *matriarchal* rule (or witchcraft in disguise). Is it any coincidence that a witch may be described as "one who constantly moves in natural or soulish power to control or dominate"? Once a demon attaches itself to such a person, the unholy combination of natural and spiritual power for the sake of domination becomes a demonic force.

    5. *Jezebel is "evangelizing" America with a media blitz of rebellion and pornography.*

It has unleashed a flood of words and images through the media to destroy the Bride of Christ through lies, slander, false doctrine, and pornography, which honors the demonic idols of old.

Consider the strongest characters in the top ten television shows. Are they male or female? Who are the smartest characters? Which gender is most consistently portrayed with more aggressive personalities and is depicted as more intelligent, resourceful, and dependable? Who really solves the problems in "TV Land" families? The women do it all, while the men take the fall as "stupid straight men" to the accompaniment of overused laugh tracks!

How many TV or movie households actually depict a healthy heterosexual marriage in line with biblical standards? (Don't hold your breath waiting to find them either.) How many programs promote abstinence until marriage and lifelong marriage relationships? How often is God mentioned without a curse word attached, and how often have you seen a genuine depiction of a minister or pastor? (I'm not counting the "ministers" who are homosexual, embroiled in steamy affairs, involved in money scams, molesting children, or drunk at the altar, or who are portrayed as spineless whiny-voiced nerds mouthing empty platitudes every time tragedy or opposition comes along.) I don't know about you, but I'm still waiting to see these things on the tube.

6. *Jezebel offers economic security and social prestige in return for worship, bondage, and domination at her hand.*

Many times Jezebel rises up in local churches or even larger organizations in the guise of powerful controlling families or power blocks. "One-family" churches often exist because one family owns the building, pays the utilities, and underwrites the pastor's salary. They usually expect to control the pastor like a puppet on a string. These controlling families or groups are often matriarchal in structure and function. In any case, their tactics are the same—they seek to control and dominate men of God for their own selfish whims. Those ministers who submit receive a measure of economic security and favor. Those who don't can suffer some painful consequences—just like Elijah of old.

Jezebel in a Dream

In other cases, Jezebel attacks from another angle. One of the most bizarre attacks I've seen came against a family that was committed to help me start the church that became Shore Christian Center. In the beginning these dear friends urged Ronda and I to start the work, and they promised to support it—financially and spiritually. When we started the church, they decided not to be a part of it. After coming to the conclusion that the gifts of the Holy Spirit were not valid for today, they decided to move out of the area. I sadly released them, although I felt they were being robbed of a wonderful part of their spiritual heritage. They told me that a "fierce battle" had transpired that had caused them anguish, pain, and many tears. They said they had to leave the area for the sake of their children's welfare and their *economic* future.

At 6:00 a.m. one morning while on a trip to Florida, I awoke in a sweat. My heart was racing. A feeling of terror filled the air, and I quickly submitted my frightening dream to the Lord. Then I went out for a walk on the Florida beach. One of God's choicest servants had once prophesied over me that God would give me the treasures of darkness and the hidden wealth of secret places, and as I gave it all to the Lord, the images from the dream began to come back to me in shocking detail.

I saw myself standing with my friends in their living room. I also heard the voice of Jesus in the room. On the wall, I saw a picture disappear as an ancient stone gargoyle appeared to take its place! This thing had a greenish tint, and it was old and moldy. It had a gothic-looking lion's head with a fish caught in its mouth. Then I heard the Lord say these chilling words: *"Your friends have gone with the power of the woman. They're having goat for supper."*

Suddenly I found myself standing before an old park fountain with water spewing from a stone configuration in the center. The bottom of the fountain was covered with stone gargoyles exactly like the one I had seen on the living room wall! Every lion's head had a fish caught in its mouth. A bronze plaque said, "Pool of Sorcery. This is the pool where witches and warlocks have come for centuries to meditate." Instantly, I felt an urgency to find my friends.

I was then whisked to another scene where the Lord handed me a club and gave me a solemn command to destroy the gargoyle images. I found myself in the basement of a particular church where I had once served as pastor. As I entered the chancel, I gasped when I saw grotesquely carved figures peppered all over the sanctuary walls! With supernatural energy, I began to annihilate those images of evil declaring, "How dare the kingdom of darkness try to take my friends and take captive the house of God!" It was at that point that I had awakened in a fever before beginning my walk on the beach.

I quickly left the beach and returned to my room for my Bible. The first thing I turned to was Exodus 23:24, which says, "You shall not worship their gods, nor serve them...but you shall utterly overthrow them, and break their sacred pillars in pieces" (NAS). Then I realized that the ugly lion was the "roaring lion" who has been devouring the people of God—symbolized by the fish—throughout the centuries, and the woman referred to by God was Jezebel! She had derived her power directly from the roaring lion, satan!

I immediately began to bind this "power of the woman" prevailing over central New Jersey, but each time I fought this battle in private devotions, I would leave the battlefield in exhaustion and nausea. Finally, I had to stop the warfare in this area for the sake of survival.

Two years later, the church had grown and I shared my vision of Jezebel with an early nucleus of elders. I told them how private prayer and battle against this Jezebel principality had left me wounded, and I asked them to pray with me. Soon all hell broke loose in leadership.

Criticism and division ran rampant. One of the men prayed *alone* and developed a mysterious complication to a common cold that produced profuse rectal bleeding. He later died from the sickness. Finally we stopped binding "the power of the woman."

Five years later our leadership had matured, and we started prayerful warfare again. This time, the results were different! One special night, all of the elders and deacons were gathered in our living room. The room was alive with the power of the Holy Spirit and a sense of expectancy. Two hours later, we sensed such a release that I joked, "I feel like singing, 'Ding dong, the wicked witch is dead!' " From that moment on, the lid was "blown off" our ministry and we experienced a bountiful harvest. We have learned that real binding of wickedness is not boxing the air but fighting evil by doing the great commission.

God is raising up armies of believers in local churches who do battle together, bound to one another in well-oiled relationships with each other and with the Lord Jesus. No one is more dangerous to the Church than the lone Christian who acquires some secrets in hidden places and then runs out to hack away with his or her five-verse machete at anything that casts a shadow or moves. The good news is this: "...greater is He that is in you, than he that is in the world" (1 Jn. 4:4).

A new woman is growing up in the earth. She is not painted like Jezebel; she has all the beauty and grace of a gazelle. She is saying, "I am my Beloved's, and His desire is toward me" (Song 7:10).

Don't Tolerate the Temptress

Notwithstanding I have a few things against thee, because thou sufferest that woman Jezebel, which calleth herself a prophetess, to teach and to seduce My servants to commit fornication, and to eat things sacrificed unto idols (Revelation 2:20).

Jesus hates to see the Jezebel spirit ravaging His Bride. He came to destroy the works of the enemy, and He did it. Now the lion is toothless, but it is still doing a good job of stealing, killing, bluffing, and destroying. Most of the time, the devil's schemes succeed because believers are ignorant of his devices; they are apathetic and passive in the spirit realm; or they are separated by strife. The fact is that satan is a defeated foe who still dwells in the earth. He is the master of deception, but his devices succeed in our lives only where we give him the authority to do so, and where we give him "a place to work." There are seven keys to defeating the schemes and devices of the spirit of Jezebel:

1. Flee youthful lusts. The Bible clearly tells us how to handle Jezebel's sexual attacks. It doesn't tell us to argue or "battle" in this particular area. It bluntly commands us: "Flee also youthful lusts" (2 Tim. 2:22). Don't think you are immune to Jezebel's tactics—remember that you are not dealing with flesh and blood alone. There is a spirit involved in this kind of sexual temptation. Obey God—flee youthful lusts. Period.

2. Stay together as people of God. Preserve the bond of love, and be submitted to one another. Pray together in unity and you will prevail in the name of Jesus. Don't allow yourself to be separated from the Body of Christ for any reason such as jealousy, pride, or laziness.

3. Discern, know, and recognize the fruits and devices of your enemy! The rebellious Jezebel spirit makes men depart from their God-given gifts or vision for "more money" or more security. It makes women become obsessed with comparisons. "Well, if you're a real man, you will make more money. If you really love me, you will get a better job. If you're not going to provide what I really want, then I'm going to go to work for myself."

This spirit also affects parenting patterns. Instead of disciplining, it makes "deals" that appeal to, or manipulate, the emotions of a child: "Now honey, if you really loved Mommy, you would do it this way." It may also control by anger instead of discipline. It may also control by using the "silent treatment," which is simply a cruel form of rejection. Parents steeped in the influence of Jezebel will try to control their children even after they are married, contrary to biblical principle. The key word is *control*—whether this Jezebel spirit is working in a church, a family, or a nation.

President Abraham Lincoln was a man who sought for truth in the 1860's. He eventually accepted Jesus Christ as his Lord and Savior, but his wife dabbled in spiritism. She actually conducted a seance in the White House, and she had no idea how costly that sin would be. It seems that a spiritual power entered the White House and brought a curse with it. Thereafter, every 20 years at the time of election, the president in office would die.

A long time ago, when Ronald Reagan took office, I prayed with a group that this power over the White House would be broken (it was time for the next twentieth year). I flew to Israel and met with Derek Prince shortly after that, and he said, "I believe that our prayers were answered and that spirit has been broken." So we left Derek in Jerusalem, and the very next day we heard President Reagan had been shot. He miraculously survived his wounds, but later on the nation learned that his wife, Nancy Reagan, was a devout follower of astrology. She also disagreed with most of her husband's convictions about abortion and the Christian faith.

Where the spirit of Jezebel is operating, there will also be an inability to make decisions. Believers who are under attack may continually walk in fear and not know why.

4. Don't tolerate Jezebel or her fruits. When you become aware of this spirit's presence, get serious and mean business. You have the authority and the duty to throw out Jezebel! Jesus scolded the church at Thyatira because its leadership *tolerated* Jezebel.

5. Use your biblical weapons against the spirit of Jezebel. According to the Book of Revelation, "...they overcame him [the devil] by the blood of the Lamb, and by the word of their testimony; and they loved not their lives unto the death" (Rev. 12:11). Stand firm in your testimony of redemption, forgiveness, and adoption through Jesus Christ. Then go on the offensive with the powerful "blood of the Lamb" that strikes terror at the core of every evil spirit from satan on down!

6. Don't compromise or mix the holy with the profane. Remember the enemy's "implication" technique. The Jezebel spirit will try to get you to compromise or sin in some small way, and then it will hold this sin against you with the skill of a master manipulator to compromise your effectiveness in the Kingdom. God's servants and God's gifts are not to be profaned by willful sin and deception.

7. Don't give "place" to Jezebel. "Neither give place to the devil" (Eph. 4:27). The kingdom of darkness has no authority over believers, nor over the Church of the Lord—except where sin has been committed and hidden. Unconfessed sin establishes a legal "embassy," or place of residence, for satan or Jezebel in our lives and relationships. Satan is looking for a landing strip in your mind. Alert your control tower to refuse him landing rights.

We must avoid mistreating our wives and children, whether we are tempted to mistreat them mentally or physically, or simply tempted to reject them and shut them out of our lives. These things create bitterness and stumbling blocks. We must avoid trying to control or dominate others. Jesus rules His Church by sacrificial love, not compulsion. Who are we to deviate from the divine pattern? We need to avoid "hiding" our problems or weaknesses. It is only as we open up to God and our brethren that we can be healed and delivered. We should avoid rebellion, disobedience, and unforgiveness at all costs. These things are like cancer to us; they only steal, kill, and destroy the holy things God has deposited in us.

Finally, we need to resist the "evangelization" of the enemy-dominated entertainment media. The sexual and spiritual ideas permeating most prime time television programs figuratively have "Jezebel" stamped all over them. They promote the same godless, rebellious, selfish attitudes that the first Jezebel exhibited in the Book of Kings! The fourth chapter of the Book of Philippians tells us what God wants us to think about and consider:

> *Finally, brethren, whatsoever things are true, whatsoever things are honest, whatsoever things are just, whatsoever things are pure, whatsoever things are lovely, whatsoever things are of good report; if there by any virtue, and if there be any praise, think on these things* (Philippians 4:8).

Chapter 3

Breasts and Shields in Public Places

Male and female created He them (Genesis 1:27b).

I am happy to report that God created men and women with major differences. Unfortunately, those differences have been exploited and exaggerated out of proportion ever since Adam and Eve first fell in the garden!

Even simple differences between male and female information processing methods can lead to serious misunderstanding and separation. Men recite the "male liturgy" like it was an original thought uttered for the first time: "Women! [said with appropriate head wagging and emphasis] Ya can't live with 'em, and ya can't live without 'em!" Women quickly respond with a version of the "female liturgy" that goes like this: "Women's faults are many, but men have only two: everything they say and everything they do." (Christian women don't feel like that, or do they?)

Just Say "No" to Lobotomy

Why is it that a woman can talk on the phone with her mother for 20 minutes, and when she's finished, she can recall every word that was said (and most of the unspoken words implied between the lines)? Then she can talk for a solid 40 minutes about that 20-minute phone call! Now Bubba can talk to Mom for five minutes (that's a long stretch for the average man), and then he will answer his wife's curious probing with, "Well, Mom's good. Everything's good at home. Everything's fine, just fine. It's good—that's it. Everything's all right."

In frustration, Bubba's wife may resort to creative questioning: "Well, how's your sister, and how are the new baby and your Aunt Carri?" With effort, Bubba may actually force out some more foggy facts like, "Huh? Oh, they're good. Everything's good—yeah, everything's good." By this time, Mrs. Bubba is certain that the man she married 12 years ago accidentally went through the "Free Clinical Lobotomy" line at the mental health unit. (He didn't, he is just a man with a one-track mind.)

We need to understand how the differences between the genders have been accentuated since the fall in Eden. Frankly, I'm thankful that females are different from males because I would really get bored sitting around with a "baseball buddy" for the rest of my life. As the French say, "*Vive la differance!*" There is only one problem: Before marriage, opposites attract. After marriage, opposites attack! Marriage forces us to face our differences head-on in close quarters. When the "immovable object" meets the "irresistible force," we then have a "failure to communicate."

It's Great Comedy Material

In Genesis 2:18, God surveyed the earth He had just made and saw Adam wandering around aimlessly in the garden talking to himself. He said, "It is not good that the man should be alone; I will make him an help meet for him." Now this was the only time prior to the fall that God said something wasn't good! What happened next turned this planet upside down and provided an unending source of excitement, not to mention a good livelihood for generations of comedians, script writers, ministers, and marriage counselors.

God gave Adam a divine anesthetic, and when he awoke, the girl of his dreams was waiting for him. At one glance, he knew this creature was "bone of his bones and flesh of his flesh" (see Gen. 2:23), but they sure looked different! God had taken Eve out of Adam's side, and she was created to be a suitable "helpmeet," or Adam's "other self." Adam was complete in himself before Eve, but he was lonely. When Adam looked at Eve, he thought, *This is my completion.* This is why men and women need one another—we are not complete without one another.

Breast-fed Families

God Himself possesses all the masculine and feminine characteristics of mankind, and He said, "I will make man in My image" (see Gen. 1:26). When He made Adam, the man possessed both masculine and feminine characteristics, but he was alone. So God took His perfect creation to a higher level of perfection by "dividing" him. God was saying, "I'm going to separate your feminine side from you, and I will give it to Eve. You are the shield, the protector. She is going to be the nurturer, the one who will be the breast." The truth is, there is great value in the differences between men and women because God made us that way. God wants man, His created "shield," to protect, lead, and guide. He wants woman, His created "breast," to continually provide a flow of His grace to her husband and children through her feminine nature. God is not ashamed to call Himself "God the Holy Spirit," the

paraclete, or Helper. Man of God, your wife is called to be
your helpmate, not your helpmaid. She is to adapt herself
to the dream that God has given her man. God calls Himself a helper. There is nothing condescending about being
a helper!

The terms *shield* and *breast* are the first two names God
gave Himself to help man understand His nature. The Bible reveals over a hundred names that God uses to describe His nature and character. If we want to know what
God is like, then we need to learn His names. Of all the
names God gives us, there are certain functional names
that He gives preeminence over the others.

God told Abraham, "Do not fear, Abram, I am a *shield*
to you; your reward shall be very great" (Gen. 15:1b NAS).
God doesn't choose words lightly. He was clearly stating
that He was going to be Abraham's protector or *shield*. A
shield is used to fend off mortal blows. It is placed between the intended victim and a mortal enemy. It receives
the blows meant to destroy the victim, and a shield is
nearly always damaged in the process. It must be repaired
if it is to remain useful in later battles. King David also
wrote by revelation, "But Thou, O Lord, art a shield for
me" (Ps. 3:3a). Throughout Scripture this biblical name of
God is also applied to His people. Adam was created in
God's image, and men are ordained to be shields to those
in their care, just like their Creator.

> *And when Abram was ninety years old and nine, the
> Lord appeared to Abram, and said unto him, I am the
> Almighty God...* (Genesis 17:1).

The second name God gave Himself was "God Al-
mighty," translated from the Hebrew *El Shaddai*. This
feminine idiom means "all-sufficient God" or "many-
breasted God." The *shield* reveals the masculine side of

God, and *El Shaddai* reveals the feminine side of God. A derivative of *shaddai* is "breast." *Shaddai* signifies "one who nourishes, supplies, and satisfies." And God is saying the He is everything represented by a woman's breast! Does that mean God is feminine? No, He is masculine in gender, but being masculine also includes feminine characteristics.

In Genesis 17, the great "reproduction chapter" of the Bible, God was about to establish His covenant with Abraham. He identifies Himself with barren Sarah, whose miraculously-opened womb became the channel God would use to bring the promised Seed, Jesus Christ, to earth many generations later to a manger in Bethlehem.

We are living in an age that says, "Don't give too much of yourself to your family; you have your own wants, needs, and desires. Get fulfilled 'out there.'" The problem is that women aren't getting fulfilled "out there"! In fact, they are dying "out there" because they've left God's place of appointment and blessing! Breast cancer is on the rise, and all kinds of diseases that have afflicted men through the years are now showing up in women because they're leaving their designated area of protection under God. This doesn't mean a woman can't work, but if it comes down to a choice between the careers of a husband or a wife, then God's way must prevail. If a husband says, "Honey, I've got to make this move," and she says, "Well, you go on and move without me, because I love my career more than I love you," then something is seriously out of order.

Nukies and Amazons

God wants to build our society on anointed "shields" and "breasts," men and women who are powerfully fulfilling their potential and destiny in Christ. Nothing is more powerful than the presence of shields and breasts in public places and in homes throughout a nation. However, our public places are currently filled with "Nukies and Amazons"!

Don't close the book yet! Have you ever seen a 40-year-old man throwing a tantrum or criticizing his wife or children in public? Have you seen grown men acting like children in the presence of a young woman, or cowering before a domineering wife? You probably have, and those men were following in the glorious footsteps of King Ahab. They might as well have climbed into a baby carriage and started sucking on a "Nukie," a baby pacifier! These aren't men—they are immature boys in grown men's bodies! They are not shielding and protecting their families because they are insecure and unfulfilled. God wants to take away their Nukies and put a sword in their hands.

The 1960's launched the "era of the Amazons" in American culture. The Amazons were a legendary matriarchal culture composed of warlike women who would cut off their right breasts so they could handle a bow and arrow more effectively. These women were willing to defy their natural physical makeup and mutilate their bodies to fill a role that was normally held by men in other cultures. Men were only allowed to live among them as utilitarian sexual "pollinators." All unnecessary males were killed or enslaved for manual labor. Leadership roles and warfare were reserved for the female warrior class. Is it any wonder that the Amazon has been a symbol of the feminist movement? Our ungodly culture continually urges women in America to "cut off their breasts" by abandoning their natural instincts and responsibilities as nurturers of their husbands and children. American society is producing "Amazons" and "Nukies" in growing numbers, and they are living proof that God was right! They are some of the most bitter, unhappy people in America! Unfortunately,

they are also producing another generation of very confused, angry, and love-hungry children. It is time for a
change!

Men need a source of nourishment and healing. It's
not within us to heal ourselves. We desperately need healing and restoration from outside of ourselves because our
shields get damaged as we function in our manly roles.
Women have the capacity and the God-ordained qualities
to provide healing, yet they also need the unique protec-
tive function of man. They need our shield for protection
and covering.

I once received a letter from a woman who wrote:

> "Since many men have not taken the challenge of
> being the head of the household seriously, [women]
> have had to accept the responsibility. By your de-
> scription of attributes associated with manliness, we
> have become men. The most difficult adjustment
> I've had to make, now that I am married to a real
> man, is remembering how to be a real woman.
>
> "My first impulses are to take full control of every
> situation. I'm hesitant to trust my husband to take
> control without my telling him to, which has caused
> many misunderstandings and duplicate arrange-
> ments. Thank God he understands my misplaced
> insecurity. He is patiently showing me that I can de-
> pend on him to be the head of our household. The
> most rewarding blessing in reclaiming my ap-
> pointed role is the delight I see in my husband re-
> acting to my femininity. It makes me feel more
> beautiful than I ever have before."

That's a powerful statement. Co-dependent, bossy
women are robbing their men and themselves of the perfect relationships God has planned for both genders. Men

are being mothered and emasculated, and mothers are being mutilated and made into men! I pray that women will learn to let go and let God, and that the men will come to the Lord and take the reins of leadership before the cart gets away!

God ordained that males and females need one another for wholeness. Look at the way God, in His creative genius, designed women to nourish from the moment of conception. While a child is in the womb, a mother provides for her baby's life resources from her own blood. Once her baby is born, her body produces breast milk that contains nourishment and a full complement of antibodies to protect the baby from disease. Meanwhile, she continues to nourish and heal the man who is her shield. He brings her security so she can raise their infant in an atmosphere of emotional health and stability.

Now men differ from women in both their physiology and temperament. They are made for confrontation and for contesting. It may not be "politically correct," but it is the way boys are made. No matter what we do, they will be that way until they become men. And they will only be fulfilled as men as they walk in their God-given function of shield and protector.

If you emasculate a man and deprive him of his God-ordained nature and role, then he will forever wonder just who he is. He will become a sick misfit in society. Men are physically suited for conflict, and we can't change that, no matter what our skewed society tries to dictate.

Educated "Suckers"

The public school system doesn't recognize this fact, and they are producing "Nukies" and babies instead of young men. Elementary schools across America have created an environment for learning that is almost exclusively feminine. Remember, we don't have male mentors any-more. Little boys are dominated by the female authority figures in their classrooms (and Sunday school classes are no different). If there is no male role model at home, then a little fellow will grow up being unsure about what "being a man" is all about.

One pastor lamented, "If only we had more slingshots and frogs in Sunday school, we would have a lot more men in church later." What was he saying? He was ac-knowledging the fact that little fellows need something to identify with, something that is distinctly "boy." The stats are out. Only one-third of all members in local churches in the United States are men! Why? Church is just another place that reinforces the "quieter feminine behavior," and punishes or disapproves of typically louder and rowdier masculine ways.

Twentieth century humanism and feminist philosophy will not change God's Word. "Well, can't we at least im-prove upon it a little bit? I mean, do I detect a little male chauvinism here?" Not at all. If Christ is our model, then we need to radically rework our understanding of gender roles, but we don't need to change God's Word! One gen-der is not to "lord it over" or dominate another—they are to serve one another. The man may need to yield his body and shed his blood to protect the woman he serves. She uses her blood to sustain and nourish the man's seed that is conceived within her body. The woman nourishes. She is the breast of the family, and it's always within her to keep giving life. From her comes a flow of the milk of God's graces for her husband and for the healing of her children.

Real Men Give Blood

The man who guards his family may have to shed his blood so his family can live. He is also designed to be the economic protector who builds and provides shelter, procures food, and obtains all the raw materials necessary to maintain a successful home. He is also expected to comfort his wife and give her emotional security.

God has called us to talk, to communicate, and to be one with our wives. If that means you have to shut off the television, then throw away the can of soda in your hand and do it. It is time to relate to your "other self." You are not going to find your personal fulfillment in the tube, in religion, or anywhere else. God has destined you to be one with the marvelous feminine creation He has placed in your life! Men have walked away from that like they've walked away from so many things. It is very difficult for us to express things that are very meaningful to us. We feel them, but we have a hard time articulating them. God says to us, like He told Moses, "I'll give you the words." God will teach you how to communicate as you fulfill your role and provide emotional security for your wife.

Mother Terminator on Call

A man is restored through the healing ability God planted in a woman. Although she is essentially non-confrontational, it doesn't mean that she never confronts. I'm thankful that my wife gets rough sometimes. She can confront wrong, and I appreciate that side of her—when it is directed toward somebody else. In general, it is not in a woman's nature or makeup to be confrontational, even though our society has changed that. Many "modern" men get their wives to call, write the complaint letter, or drive into the office to confront the elders or whatever. These men want to send "Mother Terminator" to fight their battles because they have taken on a passive nature that has not come from God.

The Bible says that a man's wife is the chief life-giver for his sexual fulfillment. According to Proverbs 5:15, she is the sexual well from which her husband drinks and receives nourishment. She is to be his sole source of sexual nourishment and intimacy. Even in the sexual context, the woman is still nourishing because it is within her makeup!

Women are not designed to resist but to nourish. They need a shield and protector from birth until death. Nourishment and childrearing cannot take place in the middle of warfare, so the woman's shield does what it takes to keep her safe and secure—far from the conflict and destructive blows of the battlefield. At birth, a woman's protector is her father, and America is missing its dads. Our little daughters are growing up without fatherly protection. Later on, a woman's husband is to be her protector for life.

The Twerp Gets the Girl

Consider the modern parable of the bully on the beach. When the crude, macho, muscle-man football player makes unwelcome sexual advances toward the beautiful girl on the beach, she resists him. She is kind of attracted to him, but she detests his arrogance. She's drawn to him, but it takes something more to unlock her heart, something more than this bully's big muscles. We've seen the scenario that follows. The bully gets too forward with the girl, and though she backs away, he keeps pressing himself on her. Finally some little guy nearby—the 110-pound straight-A math major with thick glasses and the physique of Woody Allen—dares to stand up to the bully. Everyone else cowers around in a circle, watching as this scared little twerp looks into the angry face of his foe (three-feet above him), and says, "Leave her alone."

We all know what happens. In the next scene, this poor little guy is facedown on the beach, with his face buried in the sand. His lips are bleeding, his glasses are broken and dangling from one ear. And the girl...where is she? She's right there in the sand with him! She cradles his head gently in her arms and tells him in tears, "Oh you shouldn't have done it! He's such a mean bully! Are you hurt?" (As if she needs to ask.) What has happened here? Aren't women attracted to big muscles and aggressive sexuality? No, this brave little guy was doing what God created every man to do: He was defending and shielding. He unlocked the beautiful girl's heart without the muscles. Why? God planted a desire and instinct in feminine hearts to love a man who protects and lays his life down for them. When a man does not function in that role as a shield, his wife is left unprotected and emotionally insecure: "This man is not communicating with me, he's not protecting me economically, and he's not building a place for me to establish a home for our family."

Wise wives know they shouldn't press their husbands. They let God have His grace in these situations. Men are not going to walk in the model of Jesus Christ overnight. That takes a whole lifetime of unlearning and relearning when improperly trained men come to Jesus.

We've got to find ways to implement both truly masculine things and feminine things in schools and Sunday schools. When a man comes to Jesus Christ, he begins to see that the One who loves him actually gave Himself for him. It is almost as if that old "feminine side" that was taken out of man in the garden has been reawakened! The man begins to see that Jesus Christ died for him and that His body was broken and His blood was shed to protect and restore him. It unlocks the heart of man. When that happens, the man understands that being a Christian doesn't emasculate him, even though he is literally a part of the *Bride* of Christ! When a man really sees this, he will usually break, and then his emotions will break too.

Buffoons Cry Harder

I never will forget the time a big truck driver who stood 6'6" and weighed about 285 pounds came forward in a meeting at our church. When Jesus hit him, his heart melted and rivers of living water gushed out of this man! He had come up that night ready to tear me apart! He told me later, "When you said anybody who doesn't accept Jesus Christ is stupid, I decided that you were one pastor who wasn't going to be around anymore. I was going to go deck you! I came forward to punch you out, but when I got up to you, something hit my heart; I saw Jesus." The Spirit of God just melted him, and this big old buffoon just gave his heart to Jesus and started crying. Why? He saw the "protector" side of God, the shield.

Now we get this role of the "protector" all mixed up today. If someone like James Bond saves some woman's life, then he immediately takes advantage of her inborn instinct to show loyalty and gratitude and fornicates with her. If you've noticed, the story always ends after that. That sad story has been played out countless times in our society, and each time, a life of destruction comes after the act of fornication. The people wander from one partner to another like dogs in heat, and there's no fulfillment in that. God wants us to be bonded to one another properly, but that's another subject in itself.

Put the Boxing Gloves Away

A woman is given a desire and ability to serve in a supportive, nurturing role to help her husband be the shield.

He has that strong masculine drive so he can do something for his wife and family. Wives often want to dictate what that should be, but the man's mind and heart may have a divine calling to do something else. Wives must release their husbands and yield to that dream. The end result for her will be economic protection.

God has not called men and women to fight each other; He has called us to complement one another. We can't change the Word—God made us a certain way, so we need to put our boxing gloves away. Instead, we need to confront society with a new model of masculinity in Jesus. This kind of man is tough, he's rough, he knows how to wield the sword, and he certainly knows how to use a shield. He knows how to crack the whip in battle, but he is also able to lay his life down for his bride.

This kind of manhood unlocks a woman's heart and frees her to love him the way God intended love to be. That makes for strong husband-and-wife relationships, and the world is waiting for true married love to be demonstrated. By the power of God, they're going to see it in the Church that refuses to compete, fight, or play "one-upmanship" games that devalue individuals.

Are Men Brain-Damaged?

There are three areas that highlight the unique roles of males and females:

Number one: *Male and female brains are different.* Ray Mossholder tells how in 1981 Dr. Roger Sperry, a Nobel prizewinner in medicine and physiology, discovered that between the sixteenth and twenty-sixth week of pregnancy, the male fetus is immersed in a brain bath in which two chemicals are released. Those chemicals destroy many of the inner connecting fibers between the right and left lobes of the brain, thereby limiting the male's ability to function simultaneously from both sides of the brain. This process does not occur during a female's gestation, and makes it tough for men. When I first shared this discovery with Ronda, my compassionate and understanding wife said with a twinkle in her eye, "I knew it all along—brain damage! Brain damage, that's what it is!"

I have never understood how a woman can juggle so many things at one time. I've watched Ronda cook. She cuts up things while she talks away on the phone, jots down notes, and answers Isaac's constant questions! Man, that is utter confusion for me. I want to handle one thing at a time, so I can focus on it and hit my target. I don't understand all this interconnecting stuff.

There are vast differences in our brains. Men generally favor "left brain" thinking, which is more calculating and logical. Women are logical too, but most of the time they function from the right side of the brain. Still, they have the ability to connect with the left side and be in both places at once. However, when it comes to the side that deals with compassion, feeling, and intuition, they are way ahead of men.

What are men supposed to do? Since we are supposed to be "cold and calculating," does that mean we can't get into the Spirit or really discern in the Word of God? No, the fact is that neither emotion nor logic is a good motivator for the will of God. Only the Word of God is the motivator. Whether we are oriented to left-brain thinking or right-brain thinking, we need to say, "Lord, what does Your Word say?" There are physical differences in our brains and in the ways we think. If we fail to understand this fact, we will misunderstand one another and create problems.

Where's the Basket?

Number two: *Men and women look at relationships differently.* God recognizes this in His Word! In Ephesians 5:33, the apostle Paul wrote under divine inspiration: "Nevertheless, let each individual among you also love his own wife even as himself; and let the wife see to it that she respect her husband" (NAS). Why did Paul break up his commandment into two different parts? Why did he address husbands and wives separately? Paul had a revelation about the different needs and functions of men and women.

Men are interested in conquering. We want to win the day, but women want to share the day. When do women feel sad? They battle sadness whenever they sense that their relationship with someone is bad. When they feel ugly, lonely, or unloved, then they experience bad times. A man feels awful when he senses his own insignificance, or thinks that he's a failure. If he hasn't been out there on the cutting edge and hitting the target in his profession, then he gets "the blues."

Captain Bubba Blows It

Many Christian men are committed to their marriage, but not to their *relationship*. Men are more interested in knowing which end of the basketball court to head for, but women want to concentrate on the team meeting at the team bench. Women are committed to the relationship because that is where they live. Men look at marriage and say, "Yeah, bless God, I know God wants us together, and I'm committed to our marriage. Marriage is a goal, and we've done it. What's next?"

We throw that single dramatic statement of commitment out like an anchor, and then get busy succeeding in our *work*. Meanwhile, we leave the relationship anchored in the mud—static, lifeless, and untended. The captain is out fishing someplace else while his wife is stuck in the galley, and life becomes rather boring.

A woman says, "Hold it! I'm committed to relationship. I married you, not the marriage certificate. Pull that anchor up and take me for a cruise. The moon is out. I want to hear all the nice things you told me before I signed on for this cruise. Let's hoist the sails, chart a course, and go there *together*. Let's talk to one another! Let's relate, navigate, and communicate!" At this point good old "Captain Bubba" responds, "Hey woman, what's the problem? I told you I'm committed to this marriage...I'll see you later."

Most divorces today are granted on grounds of "irreconcilable differences." Do you know what irreconcilable differences are? They are not irreconcilable, nor are they grounds for divorce. They are simply *selfish deadlocks*! Somebody in the relationship is saying, "I won't." If you analyze every problem marriage you've heard about, you will find that once you peel away the layers of pain, you will find two hearts that really love each other. Underneath all the hurt, there are two people saying, "I really do want this to work, but I don't know how to get started. I don't know how this thing got so painful—it just seemed to get out of hand. Even now, it is torture to approach it. How do we start?"

The answer is simple and direct: "Give, and it shall be given unto you; good measure, pressed down, and shaken together, and running over, shall men give into your bosom" (Lk. 6:38a). Healing and restoration begin with giving. Wives crave love and a good relationship, and husbands crave respect. Paul tells wives to respect their husbands because that's what they need. A woman needs to be reassured by word and deed that you have time for her.

Crazy Male Drivers!

Number three: *Women tend to enjoy the process of life, but men want to accomplish the goal.* Men have a desire to go from point A to point B in record-breaking time. We're made to drive hard and wild like Jehu in Second Kings 9:20. The Bible says he drove his chariot "furiously." Men are furious to get some place fast. Stoplights, traffic lights, and crosswalks are just impositions and obstacles between us and our goal. Toll booths really irritate us.

Men and women approach life differently. Have you ever taken a woman shopping? She can spend a whole day shopping while her husband slumps in exhaustion in a chair in the mall. She can just shop and shop and talk—all at the same time of course—discussing everything under the sun, and enjoy it. Men don't shop; they hunt. I don't want to go to any store unless there is something there I feel I really need. If I have decided to go there, then I will search for that one thing until I get it, and then I'm out the door! I'm uptight and tense the whole time. "I need to find this thing—I don't like being here—I need to find it and get this ordeal over with." I'm hunting for something, not browsing.

Real Men Don't Shop

Men don't browse; they stalk and pounce. Women, on the other hand, can just walk along and look, and touch, and browse from shop to shop for hours. There is a major difference here. A husband wants to fix problems quickly and efficiently because that's his mental makeup: "Let me conquer it and leave it for another challenge." Men want things fixed, and we want to do it right away. Our wives may want a problem fixed, but they also want to be heard and listened to.

When my wife tells me about a problem, I say, "Well, hold it, honey, let me get my emotional tool box. Don't worry, if you will just listen to me, it'll all work out because

I'm 'Mr. Fix-it.' I'm made this way." Dummy me. That is not what she's asking for. Ronda is just saying, "Hey Mr. Fix-it, it will be all right. If I just knew that you would actually slow down enough to hear me, I would feel better. I am more interested in knowing that you care about me than about that stupid thing that broke. If you actually take the time to listen to me, then I will be thrilled to have you fix it. But first you've got to *fix your ears* and hear me!"

Women tend to use more of the right-brain function to enjoy the aesthetic things life has to offer. A woman takes time to smell the roses, but Bubba will walk right through the flower garden with single-minded, or left-minded, determination (and possibly bump her into the thorns) to get to his destination. God wants all of us—men and women—to take the time to build our relationships and enjoy the *process* of life, instead of just waiting until we reach the destination.

The Bible tells us to live with our wives in an understanding way (see 1 Pet. 3:7). This means God wants us to understand our differences. If we don't, there will be misunderstanding. Before you do the "man thing" and jump to a conclusion like, "All right now, we know how to handle this!" let me give three "nevers" for menfolk who want to live in peace with womenfolk:

Never Say "Nevers"

Number one: *Never tell her she's silly for the way she feels.* Proverbs 25:20 tells us that singing songs to a troubled heart is a bad thing. Don't tell her that the way she feels about something is silly. Feelings aren't right or wrong; they just "are." We have to learn to deal with that. We can't walk around pompously pointing our "coldly logical" male finger and saying, "This is silly."

Number two: *Never tell her, "Don't worry about what's up-setting you."* "Let no unwholesome word proceed from your mouth, but only such a word as is good for edification according to the need of the moment, that it may give grace to those who hear" (Eph. 4:29 NAS). When your wife is worried, that is the time to apply a good word of grace, not empty platitudes.

Number three: *Never let any negative response from her make you negative to the point where you become angry and mad, for then you have a war on your hands.* James wrote, "This you know, my beloved brethren. But let everyone be quick to hear, slow to speak and slow to anger; for the anger of man does not achieve the righteousness of God" (Jas. 1:19-20 NAS). Quick to hear, slow to speak, slow to anger. This is good advice for both parties. If we're serious about listening more closely, then as men, we will need to get more in touch with the right side of our brains, where our fibers have been nearly disconnected. Women, on the other hand, need to understand that men are basically left-brain people.

God made us this way, so let's enjoy our differences and learn to understand them.

Chapter 4

Money and Sex Go Together

Centuries ago in Scotland, any man who wanted to marry a woman would simply go and get her. Today that is called kidnapping, but in that day it was considered "courtship." The woman had no say in the matter at all—and she had to live with the guy—"Hi, I'm Bubba, your kidnapper and husband." The hopeful groom would also take along a group of his chums to help, and the bravest among the buddies who helped him kidnap the woman became his "best man." Sometimes we preserve traditions without understanding their origin.

Pucker Up and Live Longer

Dr. Arthur Sabo conducted a study for a life insurance company, and he discovered that husbands who kiss their wives every morning live about five years longer than those who do not! The study also showed that men who kiss their wives daily:

1. have fewer auto accidents

2. are ill 50 percent less of the time
3. earn from 20-to-30 percent more money than the puckerless types.

The Sabo study did not indicate what kind of benefits or disadvantages kissing had for the women. But the message is clear, men: Get busy. It is to your benefit to be a kisser. If you have to use extra-strength mouthwash, or even drain cleaner, do whatever it takes to clear up your hygiene problem and pucker up!

America is living under judgment right now! According to a passage in the Book of Isaiah, we are living out one of the worst curses in the Old Testament! "Their little ones also will be dashed to pieces before their eyes; their houses will be plundered and their wives ravished" (Is. 13:16 NAS). More than half of the men in the U.S. have divorced their wives or fail to support the women they vowed before God to protect until death. So much for the biblical wife of your youth.

Some Things You Don't Give Away

More and more Christian women are coming forward to describe how they were victimized by incest and rape. Sodomy and child molestation are becoming commonplace, and daughters raised in Christian homes often give away their virginity by age 16 or by their senior prom at the latest! Men and fathers are responsible for this defilement! The Bible says, "...I the Lord thy God am a jealous God, visiting the iniquity of the fathers upon the children unto the third and fourth generation of them that hate Me" (Ex. 20:5). "But my daddy doesn't hate the Lord!" No, but if he "hates" God's ways by not walking in them, then his iniquity will be passed down—even in so-called Christian homes.

A recent magazine article said that 85 percent of the women in prison are there because they became romantically involved with a man who used them. Their misplaced loyalty, fueled by romantic physical attachment or a desire to protect themselves or their children, got them involved in robbery, extortion, drug dealing, and a host of other crimes. Men have no idea how much women seek their identity and fulfillment in men!

Ava Gardener was a famous film actress and "sex goddess" from the past. She starred in 60 major films and had three marriages, including a marriage to Frank Sinatra. She said, "I would gladly have traded my entire career for a lasting marriage, for one good man I could love, and marry, and cook for, and make a home for, who would stick around for the rest of my life."

How could this movie star desire to give up millions of dollars and the glamour of the spotlights? It involves the key biblical principle of bonding. A woman bonds to a man through her very first act of sexual intercourse, but a man bonds to a female by sacrifice or payment. He must pay a price to "earn her love," or pay a "ransom" for his bride, just like Jesus paid a ransom for the Church!

Prove You Love Me

The biblical concept of the "dowry" is introduced in Genesis 29:15-35 with the story of Jacob, the son of Isaac, who worked for seven years to *earn the right* to marry Rachel. His father-in-law tricked him and gave him another daughter, Leah, instead, but Jacob was willing to work another seven years for Rachel! Jacob bonded to Rachel with 14 years of labor, which is an incredible proof of his bond, his love, and the value he placed on her!

Without the sacrifice, there's no bonding in the male. Leah bonded sexually to Jacob on their wedding night, but he didn't bond to her because he didn't work or sacrifice for her—and Leah spent her life in tears. We will only understand the problems plaguing modern marriages by properly defining the biblical concept of dowry. No groom in those days could claim his bride unless he brought the bride a dowry. The dowry was the "inheritance" and security for the wife and any children born in the marriage in case of divorce or sudden death. The typical dowry represented three years' earnings! Today, you would have to work for seven or eight years just to save three years' wages for the dowry before you could marry your sweetheart! Traditionally, the father has to approve a dowry before anything happens. So what does that have to do with us today?

Every young man needs to come up against someone who knows him like a book, someone who knows how he thinks. Guys don't like to mess with dads, but God has planted them between the man and the daughter. Dad knows how they think because he has been there before. He knows about the hormone agenda and what is hidden in the secret places of a young man's mind.

On Review Without a Clue

Girls are interested in boys even before the boys have a clue about what is going on. They have a dream that surfaces in everything from ancient literature to modern movies and songs: It is the dream of the "knight in shining armor." It begins with a girl's dream of a personal defender who defies death and passes through a trial by fire to win her heart and rescue her from a dragon or an impregnable castle.

Dad represents the castle that a young man must pass through to fulfill biblical standards. Dad is a girl's covering and protector. She cannot be married until her beloved becomes a man and proves himself to Dad, the guardian. Only then will Dad officially transfer to the young man his responsibility as protector and provider for his daughter. Our wedding ceremonies still require fathers to publicly answer the question, "Who giveth this woman to be married to this man?"

We've Been Had, It's Dad

Ronda's dad was a nice fellow who weighed in at 240 pounds while we were dating. Ronda had a Saturday night curfew of midnight, but I naturally tried to test the limit. Just *after* midnight, we were standing in the driveway by the fender of my '55 Chevrolet, figuring we were "kind of" meeting the curfew requirements when the porch light suddenly went on. Then this great hulk of a dad filled the doorframe behind the screen door and a voice thundered, "Ronda, what time is it?" She gulped and said, "It's 12:15, Dad." "When is your curfew, Ronda?" "Twelve o'clock." "Then what in the —— are you doing out there?!"

I didn't take the time to kiss Ronda good-bye that night! No sir, Ronda's knight didn't want to hassle the "castle" just then. I jumped in that car and hit third gear before I even got out of the driveway! Young men don't want to mess with dads. Ironically, a young woman's attitude toward her dad is very important; her suitor will watch this, and he'll pick it up in his spirit. If she has a quiet and peaceable spirit under her dad's authority, then he will see an irresistable beauty in her! Every young man secretly longs for respect in his life, and he will even storm a frightening "240-pound castle" for that kind of beauty. I did it, and I'd do it again for Ronda! Women who possess the quiet and peaceful spirit described in First Peter 3:1-6 become irresistably beautiful to males.

When men don't understand how they bond to their wives, they try to bond the wrong way. We conquer and spoil them instead of work for and ransom them. Sex before marriage destroys manhood because its major function is to shield and protect, not uncover and rape.

> *Keep your way far from her* [the adulteress]*, and do not go near the door of her house, lest you give your vigor to others, and your years to the cruel one; lest strangers be filled with your strength,* **and your hard-earned goods go to the house of an alien** *... Drink water from your own cistern, and fresh water from your own well. Should your springs be dispersed abroad, streams of waters in the streets? Let them be yours alone, and not for strangers with you. Let your fountain be blessed, and rejoice in the wife of your youth. As a loving hind and a graceful doe, let her breasts satisfy you at all times; be exhilarated always with her love* (Proverbs 5:8-10,15-19 NAS).

When Soloman wrote, "Should your springs be dispersed abroad, streams of water in the street?" he was talking about semen. "Should your semen be flowing down other streets?" No, it should be channeled in the wife of your youth. Premarital sex or adultery in marriage brings an economic judgment on men. Now I'd never seen this before in the Word, but it started to make sense to me. George Gilder noted in his book on wealth in America, *Poverty and Wealth*, that much of the money in America is "old money," not new money. In other words, most of the really wealthy investors started with some of "Dad's capital" from the past or from a family inheritance. Only a few are twentieth century "right now, up-to-date, new money entrepreneurs." I believe the reason is directly related to sexual immorality in America.

Purity Is Profitable

I believe an economic curse is draining away the earning power of American men today, and it is directly linked to chapter 5 of the Book of Proverbs. John Templeton, the billionaire, has walked with Christ for years. I'm sure that if he were interviewed, he would talk about his sexual ethics, particularly how he maintained godly principles through his dating stage on into marriage. Mr. Bill Walton, the late founder of the Walmart discount store chain, was listed as the wealthiest man in America year after year until his death. He too came from a very conservative Christian background, and he publically proclaimed that Jesus was his Lord. His personal net worth was estimated at over $9 billion!

What am I saying? God blesses men with economic prosperity according to Proverbs chapter 5 when they remain chaste unto the Lord and walk in their God-given function. When men break the commands of God, the protection of God is lifted and the devourer begins to consume their wealth and earning power by breaking their physical and emotional capacity to effectively protect their wives and offspring.

Love Me Now, Hate Me Later

The man who demands sexual fulfillment and gratification before marriage from the woman he is dating is sending her a clear, unmistakable message: "My sexual gratification is more important to me than being an effective shield and protector over you." You may use fancier language, but that is the biblical principle. This breeds insecurity in the woman. For the past 30 or 40 years, our culture has bombarded us with phrases like, "Go ahead, come on! Don't let anybody repress you and hold you back! If it feels good, do it, and do it now!" The fact is that

God says "No!" Don't change God; change your mind! Be renewed in your mind.

Premarital sex steals security from a woman, even after she is married. Her husband's motives were compromised before the wedding, so she will tend to look to her children and other areas of activity for her fulfillment because there has been a bonding *before covenant*. She becomes the head of the family because illicit sex has emasculated her husband. Immorality has deprived him of his God-given role of protector!

Wives who have had premarital sex with many partners usually experience serious problems that may destroy their marriages. Their husbands often discover that their wives are not bonding with them. They seem to just "take them or leave them" with unnatural casualness, which often ends the relationship in divorce. These women bonded sexually with several other men earlier in their lives. Each time they hardened their hearts a little more to protect themselves from the pain of separation from an unnatural union without covenant until they finally marry a more stable man, primarily to combat loneliness and gain economic security. One day these unfortunate husbands may wake up to discover that their wives don't really "need" them at all. They may even get "interested" in somebody else simply because they seem to offer an even better life style. (Thank God there are exceptions to all of these situations in Christ.)

An Endangered Species

What about premarital sex with a virgin? This sin unleashes terrible consequences for both the man and the woman. The spirit of lust in a selfish man exposes a young woman's mind to the *fear* of pregnancy, and it can also expose her body to the *reality* of pregnancy before she is ready. This fear of carrying an unwanted baby for nine months while being highly visible in society fuels all the talk about abortion rights and about birth control in the high schools. This is the fear of producing something *before its time*.

When a man pressures a virgin to yield sexually, he is not committed to her well-being, and she knows that instinctively. When a man penetrates a virgin woman's hymen, her God-given vision for fulfillment with a man in total commitment is broken as he binds her to him physically and emotionally in the shedding of her blood—without covenent. This sin always takes a heavy emotional toll. If the woman is a virgin, the man exposes her to the spirit of looseness (what the Bible calls "harlotry").

A "harlot" isn't some prostitute in Times Square; it is anybody who has a loose life style, which may describe about 80 percent of Americans right now. "Or do you not know that the one who binds himself to a harlot is one body with her? For He says, 'The two will become one flesh' " (1 Cor. 6:16 NAS). Where there was a co-mingling before God's ordained time with your mate, there was a spirit transfer, and that is why you still have images of the past playing fantasies in your mind. Thank God we have a remedy in Jesus Christ.

Beware the Violators

"But the one who joins himself to the Lord is one spirit with Him" (1 Cor. 6:17 NAS). A man who sins sexually with a loose woman partakes of her spirit of harlotry. At that point, God removes His protection from him and demons are able to violate his manhood. He dies in the same way that Adam slowly died because he is lawfully handed over to the destroyer according to the curse of the law.

"Liberated women" in this century have entered the economic marketplace with unhappy results. Women are taking on many male roles, but they are also suffering the same diseases and afflictions as men. Sadly, there is no economic base within marriage for them to pursue their God-given calls. God wants the man to provide that base so the woman is free to pursue her call, even if that also involves making money. The key is that she should do it out of a harmonious foundation of agreement with her husband.

This letter drives home the principles of God for our lives:

> "I was 15 years old when I lost my virginity, [but] that was not all I lost. Because I felt unattractive and underdeveloped compared to the other girls my age, I wanted to hold on to the first person that paid me any attention. I thought no one would ever love me, but he said he did. I was not an enthusiastic participant, but I felt sure that if I did not give in that he would break up with me. I was very insecure, which should have been a huge red flag telling me to stop. Instead, I turned my head and closed my eyes and allowed him to use me. I would usually throw up afterwards when I got home.

> "I continued to see this boy hoping that he would sense my discomfort and have enough respect for my feelings when I protested to end the sexual advances. He did not. He had no respect for me, and I lost all respect for myself. I began to feel I deserved my bad feelings as punishment for disobeying God. I envisioned myself with a black heart, I can still remember that vividly. I thought I could correct my mistake by making this boy my husband.

So I orchestrated a wedding. Years later I found this man still had no respect for me. As hard as I tried to make it right in the eyes of the Lord, this man chose to further demean me by having an affair.

"What it all comes down to is that God has a perfect plan for a man and woman to make beautiful love to each other. If you think you have a better plan, think again. Ephesians 5 capsulizes the road to a good life, including the relationship meant for a husband and wife. Its main ingredient is respect.

"If you are in a relationship where your self-respect is being sacrificed, or you are expecting your partner to give up their self-respect, do yourselves a favor, end it. The Lord has got someone perfect for everyone. If you stay open to His guidance, you will know when it is right. Don't be goaded or fooled into thinking that it won't matter. Learn to listen to your heart, for the Lord puts those feelings there for a reason."

This woman's insecurity led to premarital sex, and she lost her dream and God-given channel of fulfillment, while the man lost his masculinity. We take God and sin too lightly today. Although we are new creations in Christ, our minds need to be renewed. Our sexual sins have created a bitterness toward women, and that's why so many men "use" women. Men become bitter when they lose their manhood, and repentance is the only cure. We may not have to work seven years before we marry like Jacob did, but we need to honor the principle behind the dowry.

Bombs Away, Children

I'm tired of seeing satan get into our purses and our relationships. God wants to break the evil spirits that have come in through extramarital affairs. We've been raised in a culture that has bombed and pummelled us with sexual stimulation in perverse pornography, literature, and explicit movies that hammer away at biblical values and instill godless, destructive values based on selfishness and hedonism. All of this makes our children think that sin is the norm, so they adopt that way of life. We are picking up the broken pieces in the Church as the prodigal generation streams in, shattered and ravaged by the enemy.

Jesus bonded to us when He worked for us for 33 years. He sacrificed His body and blood for our hand in marriage. He bonded to His Bride, the Church, on the cross at Calvary when He gave His life for her. We bonded with Him when we "received the seed" of salvation by faith in His Word.

If you don't take the Word of God seriously, your children won't either. If you say, "Well, Mom and I are still together, and we had sex for a year before we were married," then that will pass down to your children. Someday your daughter may find herself pregnant or seeking an abortion, and she's going to break your heart. Your son may end up running around and making (not "fathering") babies all over the place. Don't say, "How did that happen? I'm a Christian dad!" Christian dads take God's Word seriously. Instead, pray, "Father, forgive me for my lighthearted attitude. I don't want to open up my son or daughter to be ravaged by the enemy."

Paul understood the ancient covenants God made with Moses and David, and he understood the transition of the old covenants into the new covenant in Christ. He wrote, "But the one who joins himself to the Lord is one spirit with Him" (1 Cor. 6:17 NAS). He also wrote:

> *Flee immorality. Every other sin that a man commits is outside the body, but the immoral man sins against his*

own body. Or do you not know that your body is a temple
of the Holy Spirit who is in you, whom you have from
God, and that you are not your own? For you have been
bought with a price: therefore glorify God in your body
(1 Corinthians 6:18-20 NAS).

Unless we begin to understand the role of demonic
warfare in this culture, immorality will continue to spread
in local churches. It is rampant, and God is saying that we
have to do something about it! Our society has not given
our children any reasons to say no to premarital sex; it has
done just the reverse. Every day we are actively encouraged by popular movies, songs, television sitcoms, and
soap operas to sleep with everyone who is willing. Then
we minimize or try to hide the painful consequences.

My Disease Is Your Disease

When I was a boy, venereal disease was a bad thing.
Today, we hear about "sexually transmitted diseases" or
"STD's," but not "venereal disease." A lot of people have
these deadly diseases, but there is no stigma attached to
them anymore. Actually, the prefix "dis" is derived from
Dis, who was the Roman god of the underworld. We need
to remember that any sexual *dis*ease has its roots in the
bowels of hell. Everything that is a "dis" stems from satan!
Yet we still have the mentality that God is a "cosmic killjoy" on some kind of mission to keep us sexually frustrated. Do you think God would give you desires just to
watch you hit a brick wall every time? No, God doesn't
work that way.

There is a transition going on. The old order is dying
out in the Church. The "old generals" have had their day
in a sense, and soon we will hear the prophetic voice of
God say, "Behold my servants, the leaders of generations
past, are dead as Moses died in his day." God has been

preparing a number of leaders in this generation to stand and lead like Joshua. Are you one of them? Our mentors gave us a lot, but they didn't give us transparency. There was a lot of "hype" with their leadership, and a lot of un-reality as well. Thank God for the reality they saw in the Spirit, but there are a lot of things our hearts cried for that they couldn't give us. Our leaders in past days often needed their relationships healed in their own families.

People scoff at God's command that we be chaste and pure, saying, "That's not fun!" But getting rid of those demons from the past isn't any "fun" either. I remember seeing Ronda ministering to an entire room of women with broken hearts one morning after I spoke on this subject. Those women wept as they told her, "Now we understand what happened to us. We've carried all of those men in our hearts, especially the first men we bonded with sexually. We didn't know how to get rid of this bondage before now."

Maximum Sex Is Best

Even the Bible tells us there is pleasure in sin for a season (see Heb. 11:25), but in the end sin destroys our emotions and bodies. God wants something much better for His creation. He has two positives behind every commandment: First, He only wants to protect us from harm. This is the reason for the times He says "No." Second, He wants to provide something good for us. I don't believe that God wants us to give in to *minimum sex* in sin. No, the God who created sex wants His Church to have *maximum sexual satisfaction*, and He personally designed sex to be enjoyed within the bonds of marriage!

The past 20 years of "sexual revolution" in this country have really been two decades of *starvation* for genuine, covenantal intimacy. Every human being desperately needs a lasting relationship. We need intimacy, and in the past, we could get that in marriage—complete with the blessing and security of our families and our home life together.

I remember our family's gatherings in the 1950's; every Sunday afternoon we had a big dinner at Grandmom Sharp's house in Georgetown, Delaware. All the uncles and the aunts would gather, with all the kids, and we would have a blast. Grandpop was the storyteller, comedian, and patriarch, and we had family. There was security and joy in that. I look back on those days with longing. Today, we think we have to have some big bucks to go someplace that is big and exciting, or that we have to go to some new kind of movie. Yes, I enjoy those things, but I would give almost anything to go back to one of those Sunday afternoons with Grandpop to have a blast in the security of that family!

Fractured Fantasy Families

Modern society has managed to break all of that up. Parents confidently say, "Well, kids are strong. They can weather it." No, they can't "weather" it. Nearly every one of those broken young ladies with Ronda had been separated from her mom or dad through parental desertion, marital infidelity, or divorce. I'm not trying to condemn anyone, but if you were married and it wasn't in covenant, or if you have been remarried, then at least start over with a solid foundation. Successful marriages don't happen by osmosis. You have to learn how to live together in covenant. It takes hard work and labor in the Word of God. It takes trial and error, but it's worth it, for God has called us to this task.

Paul gives us the success formula for battling sexual temptation. It is almost too simple to believe: "Flee from sexual immorality" (1 Cor. 6:18 NIV). There aren't many options left for a teenage girl who is pregnant, and none of them is pleasant. Psychologists and educators have been wondering why teenage girls often want to commit suicide in far greater numbers than boys after the break-up of a relationship. One report in Josh McDowell and Dick Day's *Why Wait?* brought some amazing facts to light, and I quote:

> "It was found that when a woman goes into labor the muscle contractions trigger a nurturing instinct in the mother that makes her want to protect, love and nurture whatever passed through the birth canal....
>
> "...when a woman has relations with a man, the sex act in orgasm causes those same muscles to contract. With the contractions, the same instinct is triggered to love and nurture whatever passed through that opening."

In this case, the person involved is not a baby but a man. You see, no amount of new feminine philosophy will change God's order of creation. The woman was designed as *shaddai*, the breast. She will bond to the first man to penetrate. In a sexual affair, a woman's feelings run deeper than a man's because a deeper set of feelings is tapped—feelings that go beyond mere emotions or intellect. The study concluded:

> "Once those [female] feelings are activated it becomes all the more devastating if the relationship ends. If a woman's primal instincts to love and nurture are triggered every time she engages in sex, then conversely, every time such a relationship ends she must re-program herself to ignore those deeper feelings of longing for that man, the object of those reactions and move on to someone else. This is more than just breaking a habit, it involves

playing with biology and deep primal urges. For a woman who has had, say, 10 affairs over a 5-year period, that's 10 times she's had to train herself to ignore those nurturing instincts for the previous man in her life."

It's the Real Thing, Baby

If God destined these strong built-in feelings to be the glue that holds together marriages and families, then each affair, each lesson in negating those feelings, weakens the bonding power of the marital and familial emotions. The result is obvious in view of the divorce rate in our culture. After all, how is the body supposed to know the "real thing" after so many times of being conditioned to reject feelings of attachment? Several years of this kind of negative conditioning can destroy the glue intended to bond a woman to her husband. What is left to hold the relationship together once the glow of the honeymoon fades? By the same token, this also affects the family.

"If the nurturing instincts were meant to bind a mother to her children, yet through a series of premarital sexual affairs she's destroyed the power of the feelings, it will affect her ability to nurture her children as well."

This helps explain the abnormally high incidence of child abuse, abortion, and abandonment in our society. The "love generation" of the 1960's did it all in the name of love. They scrapped God's plan and launched a "sexual revolution," seeking intimacy. They thought they were going to find it in promiscuity, but in reality they came to the end of themselves emotionally. Now we know it hasn't worked and that it doesn't fulfill us. Why? God has made a contract forever; He says marriage is blessed and the bed is undefiled (see Heb. 13:4). It is the only place for true sexual fulfillment.

Fathers in the Church need to take a stand again as shields, and mothers need to again become the *shaddai* for a new community that is born in the Spirit and led by the Word. We need to declare: "God, by Your grace we'll teach our children how to walk in Your truths. We'll bind them to our eyes; we'll make a a covenant with our eyes and with our hearts."

Ancient Art Restored

A top salesman for an insurance firm was to reveal the secret of his success, and everyone there already knew it certainly wasn't in his appearance or personality. Most of the high-powered salespeople there thought he looked like a loser, but the numbers didn't lie: He was doing something right. Finally he told them, "When I started in this business a few years ago, I had a friend who was really successful. He gave me a bit of advice, and all that I've ever done is just follow that advice." Everybody leaned forward, anticipating the motivational tidbit he was about to reveal. Then he continued, "What my friend told me was this: 'You can get a man to do anything you want him to do if you only listen to him long enough.' "

Now if that is true in sales, how much more should the people of God *listen* until we know what God is really saying? Then we can not only become healed ourselves, but we can also listen until we really understand the needs of our wives and our children!

In a recent poll, 75 percent of the men contacted told pollsters their marriages were all right, but only 25 percent of their wives gave that response! That means 50 percent of those wives believed their marriages weren't all right and their husband didn't even know it! Why? We're not listening to each other. We're living in a culture that doesn't want to listen. In colonial days, people would lay the foundation of listening skills for learning. The old sermons often lasted two, or two-and-a-half, hours. Current church growth statistics tell us that you can't really have a booming megachurch if the pastor speaks much over 35 minutes, unless of course, it's a "faith" church (the Word of Faith people are different in this area as their spiritual hunger seems greater).

The Theory of Devolution

Humanity isn't getting any better. We still face the same problems we faced after the fall in Eden because we haven't returned to God's Word. Ed Cole says, "A cannibal hasn't become better just because he now has a knife and a fork." You have to change the man within. You can dress up a pig with ribbons and jewelry. You can put perfume on it, but it's still a pig. After you clean that pig up and let it go outside, it will head straight for the mud! We were the same way until Jesus entered our hearts. He is the only One who will take care of sin. He's not saying, "I've given you the ten invitations." He's saying, "I've given you ten commandments."

Nothing but the blood of Jesus can take sin away. Don't rely on some new self-help course or the latest pop psychology fad; and don't try to find divine forgiveness on the couch of some psychiatrist. Dr. Carl Menninger wrote a book in the last decade before he died entitled, *Whatever Happened to Sin?* It is a prophetic message for clergymen. While we are hiding behind pompous talk about problems, desires, and "irresistible" biological needs, God says, "You bunch of phonies! I have provided a way out for all of that. Just tell the people the truth: call sin, sin." God knows what He is doing. Man whitewashes, but God washes white.

Where Is Your Daughter?

When I get my eyes on Jesus, I don't look at the harlot on Fifth Avenue and say, "You disgusting thing." When I was in Los Angeles, I saw girls who were 13 or 14 years old, walking around trying to turn somebody on. I said, "My God, that's somebody's little girl." Another pastor recently reported that a man in his congregation went to another city and called a number for a prostitute service. When the prostitute came to his room, it was his daughter! I thank God in Christ Jesus that there are great endings, and that story had a great ending. That father and daughter are together now as a family. God has healed them and set them free!

A little fellow came in one afternoon with his face covered with gooey ice cream stains. He announced, "Mommy, I had two ice cream cones today!" She asked, "How? You didn't have any money. Did you steal those ice cream cones?" He grinned and said, "No, Mommy. It was very simple. I told the lady that I would like chocolate ice cream and I took it in this hand. Then I told her I would like a vanilla ice cream cone, and I took it in this hand. Then I said, 'Ma'am, would you get the money out of my pocket? Be careful that you don't hurt my pet snake.' "

Leadership takes imagination. If we're going to be hard on somebody, let's be hard on ourselves! If you have won victory in a certain area, then don't look at somebody else who is struggling with it, and say, "Boy, if the pastor just knew what you did last week!" I believe God's going to help us build imaginative bridges to reach this society, not condemn it.

Chapter 5

Safe Sex

Now we're going to talk about sex, so say to yourself, "I'm embarrassed already." This chapter will give you an edge with your spouse, your friends, and even your enemies. When they ask, "What are you reading about?" just tell them, "Sex." When their eyes light up and they ask to borrow this book, tell them to buy their own, or just tease them with choice tidbits from your favorite section. Life might get exciting.

Husbands, love your wives, just as Christ also loved the church and gave Himself up for her ... Nevertheless let each individual among you also love his own wife even as himself; and let the wife see to it that she respect her husband (Ephesians 5:25,33 NAS).

Paul completed his message on family life saying, "Put on the full armor of God, that you may be able to stand firm against the schemes of the devil" (Eph. 6:11 NAS). God's people are "for" good things and "against" the works of the devil. God gave us a clear and precise word, sandwiched right between murder and thievery: "Thou shalt not commit adultery" (Ex. 20:14).

Love After Surgery

Step into the garden, and let your imagination run wild (I know you're not used to it, but do it anyway). What happened to Adam when he first saw Eve? Did he smile? Did he whistle? We don't know, but we do know that he had been in the garden picking berries and talking to animals just a short while before.

Adam had something deep within him that he wanted to share with somebody else, but nothing he found quite filled the bill. Then God came on the scene said, "Hey Adam, do I have a surprise for you! I've been waiting for just the right moment, and now is the time. Adam, I want you to take a nap. When you wake, you are going to have a surprise."

When Adam woke up, he saw a living, breathing, shapely, and, if you will, very sexy, long-haired beautiful Eve. That must have been a refreshing contrast to the baboons! The Living Bible says Adam's first words were, "This is it!" (Gen. 2:23a) He went on to declare, "This is now bone of my bones and flesh of my flesh; she shall be called Woman, because she was taken out of Man" (Gen. 2:23 NAS). He was seeing something he had never seen before, and it delighted him immensely!

God Is Pro-Sex

Some people are shocked to learn that sex was God's idea. He wove the sexual dimension of our personality into the very fabric of our being. We are sexual beings physiologically, psychologically, and sociologically. We are created as sexual beings, and sexual attraction is no accident! Don't believe the Victorian myths—God has ordained it this way! God talked to Adam and made a helpmeet to help him in his lonely state long before there was ever any mention of procreation. Marital companionship and sexual union were all in His plan to end Adam's isolation with incredible joy!

Don't fall for the lie that sex is just for procreation. That old Victorian myth is a lie of the enemy. Some Bible commentators believe that the romantic and openly erotic language of the Song of Solomon actually describes Adam's feelings when he first saw Eve. God's blatantly pro-sex stance can be seen all through the Bible, though, and not just in the Song of Solomon.

Healthy Lovers Are Never Too Busy

Over the last decade, I've seen an alarming increase in the number of young married couples who come to me for counseling because their lives seem to be falling apart. Most of these couples shared a common problem that was pinpointed by this personal and intimate question: "Are you regular, are you consistent in your romantic love for each other?" Generally, they would tell me something like, "Well, we've gotten very busy. Uh, we may make love once a month." A lot of them say, "Gee, it's been like two or three months now." Most of the serious problems in their relationships tended to have begun at the same time they started to withhold their marital love, intimacy, and support from one another. Everything else seemed to crowd in on these young couples, and the first thing they sacrificed to circumstance was their love and intimacy with one another.

Satan wants to come against us in this area. He is not a sexual being, but he knows that something about it reflects the image of God and honors Him. He hates human sexuality, so he tries to pervert it. The father of lies has created all kinds of myths in our culture so we cannot deal with sex properly. The only solution is to return to God's

Word to see what He has to say about sex. Listen, the world has been getting sorry advice from Donahue, Dr. Ruth, and Hugh Hefner. I believe it's time for the world to get the real story from the Church of Jesus Christ!

Marriage: The Lust Buster

We're living in a sex-saturated society that seems to live by the motto, "Thou shalt lust in thought, word, and deed." In 1970, a pivotal movie called "Love Story" swept across America's theaters, and millions of people watched as Jennifer and Oliver "fell in love" Hollywood style. Instead of a marriage, they had a "meaningful relationship," which means they had sex without the benefit of vows, commitment, or the inconvenience of morals. After that, a deluge of people decided to live together without taking the vows of Holy Matrimony. The basic philosophy was simple: "Well, if our relationship is 'meaningful,' then we have every right to spend the night together and have sex."

We kind of expect that from the world, but the problem is that this devilish philosophy is in the Church! It has slithered its way down the aisle and into the pulpit and the choir loft. We're not influencing the world for good; we're being influenced by the world's goods! In 1988, Josh McDowell quoted a survey that found that 65 percent of the evangelical teenagers polled had experienced some type of sexual contact before age 18. Forty-three percent had experienced intercourse. Even at the tender age of 13, 20 percent admitted that they were sexually active!

The saddest statistic of all amounted to an outright indictment of the Church: the percentage of people in the Church who were or had been involved in illicit affairs was only 10 percent lower than people who claimed no church affiliation or regular church attendance! The pollsters also asked, "Where do you get your information concerning sex? What influences you?" Fifty-seven percent of those surveyed got their information from movies, and 78 percent verified that little or no information about sex had ever been received from the Church! That means Hollywood sets the standards, whether we want to admit it or not.

The Bunnies Stopped Playing

While Christians are climbing onto the adultery bandwagon, some of the original band players are climbing off! Hugh Hefner, the founder and publisher of *Playboy* Magazine, raised eyebrows when he finally married. His wife wanted to make some changes around the mansion (she wasn't thrilled about nude women coming into her home and walking around her husband). I remember hearing that Hefner said, "Wouldn't it be neat if my life became a symbol of the conservative decade ahead, just as it was a symbol of the swinging sixties and seventies?" His wife, Kimberly Conrad, said, "I want this to be more like a real home. The girls still come over but they're wearing their bathing suits. I think that's nice."

The "big bunny" has become a little stuffed toy. His casino closed, and his playmates have argued and sued one another. The chosen women have become jealous of one another, and now they've left the empire. One of Hugh's former lovers committed suicide, the key clubs are closing, and the last "Playboy Club bunny" took another job as a security guard! He is finally seeing the end of something that he thought would usher in the "Age of Aquarius," where everybody would do what they wanted with no restrictions. God is breaking up a lot of empires.

"This Life No Longer in Service"

God's will for the Church is clear. He wants this generation, His Church, to be as if it were without spot or blemish. We will never fulfill His desire unless we learn what His Word says about our sexuality. Have you ever been cut off on a telephone? The communication stops. Contact ends. When you participate in an illicit relationship, whether it is fornication before marriage or adultery as a married person, your sin breaks the connection and stops communication.

The angels of God are sent to minister to those who are to inherit salvation (see Heb. 1:14), so all of us probably have at least one guardian angel. That guardian angel ministers to you, and it helps bring the Word of God to pass as you make your godly confession in word and deed. "Bless the Lord, ye His angels, that excel in strength, that do His commandments, hearkening unto the voice of His word" (Ps. 103:20). Your angel can only respond to the words you speak that agree with the Word of God. If you're in an illicit relationship, you have become a vulnerable target for satan because he now has free access to you. Why? Your guardian angel can no longer protect you.

God commands us not to commit adultery. He is not a "killjoy," but He commands us to have one partner in a covenantal relationship because He knows all too well the deepest human hurt: a broken heart. Unless we are in line with the Word of God sexually, we will be heartbroken and heartbreakers.

Don't Be a Crackpot

Once we dropped a Hummel, a delicate German porcelain figurine, and we carefully glued it back together. It is now one piece again, but you can see all the cracks.

Some of the people I counsel have come in after their lives have been broken to pieces by sin. The Holy Spirit can put them back together, but that doesn't mean that they will forget. The memory of their pain will always be a crack that you can see upon close examination. That is why the Lord tells us to live His way: We won't have to experience the painful memory of all the cracks.

Illicit sex is not the unpardonable sin, and Jesus will forgive. But He told the woman caught in adultery, "Go, and sin no more" (Jn. 8:11). That is His word to our generation. If you have had an illicit affair, or are involved right now, then stop, repent, and sin no more. You can only do it through the power of Jesus Christ within you. "Yeah, but you don't understand: I'm single and I've got all these desires and urges! I just don't know how to handle them." Jesus Christ is your Pattern. He was single, and He "handled it." He didn't have any superpower to help Him in His days of struggle and temptation that you don't have! It's a matter of your will. Are you willing to call on God and receive strength in this area?

Our culture offers up a dazzling smorgasbord of enticing temptations, and satan constantly whispers, "Oh, come on! Take anything you want, any way you want it. Just eat and have your fill!" God knows that a life that is indiscriminate, undisciplined, unrefined, and undignified will disgrace you. God doesn't want you to be disgraced. Unbridled lust saps life, but dignity and continual renewal is found in a committed, covenantal love that lasts for a lifetime.

Prescription for Maximum Sex

God designed sexual intimacy as the ultimate release of ecstasy, but this "maximum sex" can never be experienced outside of a committed contract or covenant in marriage. Why? Maximum sex is only experienced by partners who live together in the *unbroken confidentiality* of covenant. Men and women are more than animals with bodies and hormones. They are eternal spirit beings who possess a soul and dwell in a body. Total union involves all three parts of our being. Bodies can unite almost anytime under any circumstances (just like dogs, which is what modern American sexuality seems to be patterned after). Only lifelong marriage assures that your secrets are just that: secrets between you and your spouse.

Anthropologists have found that virtually every culture exhibits an innate desire to cover their sexual organs in some way. Why? Is it because nudity is bad? It involves more than that. Every person's dignity demands the right to set limits beyond which the public cannot probe.

Total giving requires total vulnerability. The act of intimacy is designed for those who are committed. You cannot give your body to someone and then just have them leave, and pretend that nothing will harm you. It breaks you. You have threatened your ability to be intimate because you can be easily embarrassed by somebody's careless exposure of your intimate secrets for public review, critique, or ridicule. You might as well allow yourself to be paraded on stage so your loincloth can be stripped away in front of television cameras so everyone can "vote" on the value or quality of your most secret parts.

"Juicy Details at Seven"

I chuckle when I see Hollywood stars get into illicit relationships only to see their pictures and secrets spread all over *Playboy* Magazine and the papers three months later when their partners decide to make a quick buck by giving out the intimate secrets of their affairs. That usually strikes fear in any group that runs together. It also happened to a number of sports figures. When the lurid details of the indiscretions of certain married ballplayers hit the news, it sent a shock wave throughout the world of baseball. Suddenly, all the fellows that were real loose began to back off and say, "Maybe there's something to just staying with our wives and not playing around on the road. You never know. My name could be all over the billboards before I know it."

Christians can experience the highest form of sexual ecstasy known on the human level because they have God's full approval, encouragement, and blessing! "Till death do us part" is a setup for *super sex*. Marriage is God's way of preserving your dignity by maintaining your intimate secrets in a mutually respectful relationship that will endure.

There are several devilish misconceptions that consistently cloud this picture of God's plan for maximum sex. It is time to pull these strongholds down!

Number one: *The world says morality is a matter of "doing what is natural."* If it's natural, do it. If it feels good, do it. Do you believe that? For some reason, we don't buy that line in other areas of human behavior! "Well, he made me mad, so I shot him." "Yeah, I had to get the car fixed this week. I didn't have any money, so I went down the street and robbed a neighbor." That is "natural" too, isn't it? If you need money, get it from somebody—whether the person agrees or not. Did somebody make you mad? Shoot him. Hey, if you're feeling that hormone power, then go for it! No! Morality is not a matter of doing what is natural—it is a matter of doing what is right. Who cares what anybody thinks: I want the absolute. I want to know what is right, and that is found only in the Word of God.

Number two: *Marriage restricts your freedom to enjoy sex.* That is a myth. If you have sex outside of marriage, you are enslaved to guilt and you lose your self-respect. Within the marriage covenant, through the Holy Spirit, your sexual intimacy can transcend the emotional, the intellectual, and the social, to reach a place where God is in the experience! God created sex for your pleasure, not simply for procreation. What we have been erroneously taught is "taboo" is really God's free gift for us to enjoy for a lifetime!

The apostle Paul dropped a bombshell about the act of sex when he wrote to believers with unbelieving spouses, "For the unbelieving husband is sanctified by the wife, and the unbelieving wife is sanctified by the husband..." (1 Cor. 7:14). The word *sanctify* means "to set apart." You are setting your spouse apart for the blessing of God when you engage in the romantic act because it has within it healing powers. God has designed it that way. The romantic act releases the highest form of pleasure known to man, and it is only available within the boundaries of God's blessing. Marriage does not restrict your freedom to enjoy sex—it expands and deepens it!

Number three: *Partners must live together before making a marriage commitment to find out if they're really "sexually compatible."* It won't work. Without a prior commitment to see a thing through, even the least important irritations can cause you to grow apart. At the slightest sign of frustration, you can go your own way. Marriage has a different ingredient that overcomes human fickleness. It says, "We're in a contract to make this work." Even Dr. Ruth has admitted that people who live together before marriage still divorce at the same rate as those who do not. It doesn't help to fornicate before entering a covenant; it just adds guilt and shame to the marriage equation. Even the world recognizes this!

Number four: *Sex is okay between consenting adults as long as nobody gets hurt.* The problem is that somebody always gets hurt. Now I want to get personal. On December 30th, in 1967, I was on my way to Wilmore, Kentucky, to return to Asbury College. Ronda and I had made a commitment to marry at some future date. I knew that she was the one, and I deeply loved her. (I still do. That's part of the joy of being in covenant with the special one God has for your life.)

Hi—I'm Temptation

I went to Washington, D.C., to catch a plane, but when a snowstorm closed down the airport, the airline put me in a hospitality hotel, along with some other passengers and the flight crew. I went to my room, wrote a few letters, and got some food to eat in my room. When I opened the door to put the tray of dishes in the hall for housekeeping, a woman came down the hall and said, "Hi, how are you doing?" She was real friendly, and since I'm a friendly person, I said, "Good, how are you?" She asked, "Are you stuck here?" and I said, "Yup, I'm stuck here." After some more small talk, I went back in my room.

Later that evening, I went downstairs to the bookstore in the hotel lobby. I was looking at a book on a rack when somebody came up from behind, put their arms around me, whispered something in my ear, and squeezed me! I thought, *What's going on?* When I looked around, it was this young woman. She was a stewardess on my flight. When she said, "What are you doing tonight?" I answered, "Well, nothing."

"Look, some of the pilots are throwing a party upstairs, and there are some government officials there too," she said. When I said, "Uh-hum," she added the magic words, "And there is lots of food." That did it. Without thinking,

I said, "Really? I'll be there." So I went to the party and ate really well. It was great to meet new people, but I mostly remember that the food was fantastic. I knew I wouldn't be getting that kind of feast in college, so I really loaded up.

At around 1:00 a.m., I said, "Well, I'm going to head out now." Then this girl said, "Well, I am too." Then I thought, *Oh, golly, well, okay.* When I got in the elevator, I locked my eyes on the red floor lights, and as the door slowly closed she said, "I'll be down to your room in just a few minutes." Then I got that familiar lump in my throat. It's funny what you think about at those times. I kept thinking, *This is just like James Bond.* I almost wanted to practice it: "Bond's the name—James Bond."

No Eunuch Here

Then I realized just what I had gotten myself into. I thought, *Dear God, now what am I going to do, Lord?* He gave me the words, and when those doors opened, I stepped out into the hallway with her. She was a lovely young woman. I'm going to be honest: I was excited. There was a part of me that was yelling and screaming and hollering and jumping up and down. Do you think all preachers were eunuchs from birth or something? (I think that's why so many of them get in trouble; they never admit to the reality of life.)

I heard the Spirit of God talking to me at the same time she was talking. He said, "This woman is in trouble. She needs Me. And you are the one to help her." I turned to her and I knew I had the words. When I spoke, she immediately broke down and started to cry. She said, "I was engaged once, and you look like the man I was engaged to. He broke my heart then, and I've been loose since then. I am a Baptist minister's daughter, and I have run from God." I prayed with her, and she asked the Lord to forgive her. She gave her heart to the Lord again.

Avoid Solo Duets

Even with the miracle fresh in my spirit, when I went down to my room part of me thought, *Oh, you dummy!* That's the natural man, the flesh talking. God has brought that situation back to me at different times to remind me of His call. That situation was a test that God allowed to see if I could handle ministry. Now I recommend that you flee situations like that whenever possible, but sometimes you can't get out of it. I was stuck in that situation. In our ministry I don't counsel with women alone. I take Paul's advice: I let the older women counsel the younger women, or I do it as part of a team with my wife. At the very least, if I have to see a woman in a ministry situation, I make sure all the doors of my office are open and that people are here.

Somebody wanted to see me one night after a service, and it was dark in the building. I responded, "Madam, it's not that I don't want to help you, because I do. But I must check with our deacon Brother Wombough; I want Brother Bob standing right out here when I talk to you in there." When Bob agreed to stay, I told the lady I could meet with her for a few minutes.

God was testing me in that Washington hotel to see whether or not I would take advantage of somebody that had a deep need. People like that hurting young stewardess are all around us in the Christian community. God is saying, "Will I have a Church that will refuse to look at these situations as opportunities for personal advantage, that will refuse to minister the world's way? I desire a people who will go and extend My hand and be My voice, who will serve as the experience of love and salvation to a

world that's groaning and hurting." That is the only dem-
onstration that will change the world, and if we're honest
with one another, it will also change the Church. When
there is sex between consenting adults outside of their
marriage covenant, somebody will always get hurt.

Number five: *Marriage will limit my individual development.* Oh, come on. Trust, mutual agreement, and mutually agreed upon goals are the most exciting things about
life! The Bible says two are better than one (see Eccles.
4:9). Two are better than one. Now unless you're called to
be single, two are definitely better—and more fun—than
one!

If you were in a bad, uncovenantal marriage relationship that ended in divorce, I'm not trying to condemn
you. You may have walked right out of the world into the
heart of God and then found a mate who went into covenant with you because both of you were agreed in Christ.
You may have had to part because there was no peace in
your home or your lives. Perhaps you wanted with all your
heart to keep covenant, but found no way to stay in the relationship while maintaining your sanity. In such cases, I
think Paul is clear: "But if the unbelieving depart, let him
depart. A brother or a sister is not under bondage in such
cases: but God hath called us to peace" (1 Cor. 7:15).

There are other admonitions concerning believers
who were in covenant when they decided to separate.
Normally, believers in this situation are not free to re-
marry unless their situation meets certain exceptions
mentioned in the Bible, but I won't get into that.

Number six: *You need experience before the wedding night.*
I want to tell you something. My body screamed, shouted,
and yelled just like yours when I was dating Ronda, but we
had made a covenantal commitment to one another and
to God that we would wait until our wedding night. As a

result, God has blessed us abundantly with ecstasy secrets that we will never divulge to anybody. It just gets better and better as the years go by! The experience that we really need before marriage is the experience of keeping our word and honoring a holy covenant!

If you're a young person, you need to practice one word: "No." Statistics state that three out of every four college girls have already lost their virginity. Those odds are high. Say "no" and enjoy the ecstasy that only comes when you do things God's way. There is a first time for everything, and the best place for sex is on your honeymoon. Believe me, you will never forget the first time. Launch a lifetime together. Christen the ship. It's ribbon-cutting time. Do it without guilt, without fear, and without shame. The excitement will just keep growing!

There are some things—the most important things—that you just cannot partake of until God's proper timing. I don't care what the world's secular psychiatrists are saying. Their offices are filled with brokenhearted people who have been damaged from deviation from God's plan. Their only cure is in Jesus Christ. Learn to say "no" until the wedding date, and then experience ecstasy of the blessing of the Lord.

Jump the Ditch

The seventh commandment is also designed to keep families whole and marriage relationships healthy. If your marriage relationship is in a rut, then get out of it! Rock the wagon and work together to steer your marriage to new places as a team. "Sweetheart, we've got to relate again. Let's negotiate this obstacle together. Let's work as a team to get this thing rolling again! Let's talk, let's dialogue, and how about going on a hot date with me tonight?" Take that woman out on the town and buy her that favorite meal at her favorite restaurant. Give her some class, and make her feel like a million dollars. She is your glory, man of God. Paul is clear on that in First Corinthians 11:7.

Have a special date night. I look forward to that one night a week when we have a date. It's good. We still go to the beach, and we still like to go under the boardwalk once in a while. I can just hear the media, "There he is! We knew it. We've been following this preacher around, and now we caught him with a woman all right!" "Dingbat! This is my wife—the greatest woman on earth! That's who I'm under the boardwalk with." Hallelujah!

Here are some guidelines for successful marriage relationships:

Number one: *Only marry another Christian.* The Word of God clearly says, "Be ye not unequally yoked together with unbelievers..." (2 Cor. 6:14). I thank God that He pulls through some of those who have violated this warning, but it is better to follow the Word of God. You will avoid 98 percent of the problems people face.

Number two: *Commit your marriage to Jesus Christ.* If you haven't done this before, do it today. Hold her hand and say, "Let's make Jesus Christ Lord of this marriage."

Number three: *Make a commitment to improve your marriage.* Commit to improve your relationship. Go on dates. Listen to marriage-enrichment tapes together. Learn more about what God wants in terms of improving your marital life.

Number four: *Make your spouse a priority.* Pray, "Lord, what does she really want to do?" and then talk with her about it. Don't just ask yourself what you want to do.

Number five: *Meet your partner's sexual needs.* Don't refrain from the marriage bed to get your way. Meet her needs, and you won't have to worry about her looking elsewhere. As a pastor, I want to see a sexually vibrant people! When people ask me about our church, I want to say, "Oh, yeah, we're sexually active! Yes, indeed, boy, we're an active congregation, but it's safe sex!" Hallelujah.

Number six: *Avoid relationships that may lead you to an affair.* If you are really close to another couple, but you notice that your eyes wander and your mind lingers, then *flee youthful lusts!* Deal with it. You may have to break off a relationship for a season.

Nothing Left But Sex

At a Golden Wedding Anniversary party, two little grandsons innocently asked their grandparents, "Grandma, Grandpa, what did you do when you were young to not get disease?" Grandma took her ring off and held it up so they could see it. Then she said, "This." That's the answer. When God's laws are obeyed, there are no worries about syphilis, gonorrhea, AIDS, or herpes. All that's left is just clean fun: pure, unadulterated, Holy Ghost-filled sex.

Martha attended a luncheon with ten other women, and during the conversation, one lady boldly asked how many of others had been faithful to their husbands. Martha later told her husband that only one woman raised her hand, and added, "It wasn't me." But then she quickly said, "I have been faithful to you, though." Her puzzled husband asked, "Well then, why didn't you raise your hand?" Sheepishly she answered, "Because I was ashamed."

Faithfulness and fidelity are actually branded as shameful in our upside-down world. We're living in twentieth century, post-Victorian free-love America. So affairs are in. Statistics vary, but most experts now say that two-thirds of all married men, and half of all married women will commit adultery sometime during their marriage. Bill Hybels credits Dr. Albert Ellis, a prominent sexologist, with coining the term "healthy adultery" to describe the counsel he gives couples whose romantic lives have faded. He actually urges them to "commit adultery so that they can rejuvenate their relationship"! God is emphatic: "Thou shalt not commit adultery." There are no conditions and no escape clauses.

How can we "affair-proof" our marriages? The answers are simple and direct:

Number one: *Affair-proof yourself.* You and I will each stand and give an account to God for what we have done with our lives. We will all be tempted; it's part of our human nature. What are you going to do with temptation? Will you nurture it or attack it? Attack the thought. I was talking with a man who said, "You know, I've had my chances, but I love God, and I love my wife so much that *it has made me run* from situations. I can see past the pleasure fantasy to the pain." I appreciate that. Play the pain to nullify the tempting pleasure of sin.

Number two: *Affair-proof your spouse.* In other words, as Bill Hybel says, "keep your lawn so green that all others look brown." It is important for you to affirm your spouse so much that she knows nobody could ever love her the way you do! "Somebody else may be better looking, make more money, or have more abilities and gifts than me, but honey, they could never love you the way I do because we were called to be together!" Now that creates security. Affair-proof your spouse. Why trade a Corvette for a pair of Rollerblades, or a Harley for a bicycle?

Number three: *Affair-proof your life style.* Most extramarital affairs happen between close personal friends or co-workers. Make sure that your friends are strongly committed to improving their own marriages. Avoid long phone calls to special friends of the opposite sex, and avoid taking lunches alone with them. Many Christian businessmen go to lunch accompanied only by their secretaries. This is a deadly seedbed for unhealthy relationships. Secular businesses often link a male with a female and fly them off somewhere to do some business. This is wrong.

Number four: *Communicate.* Man of God, ask your wife to read this paragraph about male/female communication.

For Women Only: *When you want to get your husband's attention, don't try talking to him. Move in close, put your hands on his head, and look into his eyes. They are probably glazed, but don't panic! Just say, "Testing, testing, testing. Ronda to Dewey* [plug in the appropriate names]*, Dewey, are you in there? This is Ronda. Testing." Once the glaze begins to go, you can start to communicate. It will work. Now all of the times you yell, "You don't love me, you just sit there in front of that thing watching through to the ninth inning! I don't care who Ken Griffey is!" He doesn't even hear that. But this will work. Go ahead and try it. You've got to get the eyes moving again to land the attention of the man.*

Single people can start affair-proofing early by entering marriage in purity. God didn't arbitrarily decree that half of the human race would live in sexual frustration, and the other half gets a blank check. He knows that we are designed so that any type of sexual activity will lead us to a "merging." That's why you cannot hold the hormonal accelerator down and apply the spiritual brakes at the same time—something will pop. It's human to hug and kiss. It's human to embrace. But when you start engaging in petting, your body is designed and equipped to complete what you started. Don't start it so you won't have to fight it. Wait until you are in a marriage covenant with a partner that God has given you for a lifetime of ecstatic love-making before lighting the fire! Now that is *safe sex.* Even better, that is *maximum sex, the way God intended it*!

Chapter 6

Eight Marks of a Man in Boxer Shorts

Congratulations, you're male. What do you have to show for it? You are the favorite target of situation comedy writers, comedians, rabid...er...radical feminists, stress, and cancer. Compared to your female counterpart, you are six times more likely to be arrested for drug abuse, nearly nine times more likely to be a drunk driver, and eight times more likely to be arrested for a serious crime.

Cheer up, mister. If you don't end up in prison (you are 25 times more likely to land in federal or state prison than a woman), at least your life expectancy is only seven years shorter than a woman your age. Unfortunately, if your VCR has been stolen recently, the odds are 12 to 1 that it was stolen by a...well, you already know. So much for gender solidarity.

Spring Cleaning at God's House

What about the man who wears boxer shorts? Well, that's a different story (if there is more to the man than the shorts). Jesus was different, and although He lived and ministered before there were Fruit of the Looms, there has never been a man who is His equal:

Then it was time for the annual Jewish Passover celebration, and Jesus went to Jerusalem. In the Temple area He saw merchants selling cattle, sheep, and doves for sacrifices, and money changers behind their counters. Jesus made a whip from some ropes and chased them all out, and drove out the sheep and oxen, scattering the money changers' coins over the floor and turning over their tables! Then, going over to the men selling doves, He told them, "Get these things out of here. Don't turn My Father's House into a market!" Then His disciples remembered this prophecy from the Scriptures: "Concern for God's House will be My undoing" (John 2:13-17 TLB).

What happened to the "Prince of Peace"? Didn't Jesus say, "Blessed are the meek…"? So what got into Jesus in the Temple? "And His disciples remembered that it was written, The zeal of Thine house hath eaten Me up" (Jn. 2:17). The Bible says Jesus acted out of *zeal*, zeal for His Father's house.

When Jesus arrived at the rabbi's home and saw the noisy crowds and heard the funeral music, He said, "Get them out, for the little girl isn't dead; she is only sleeping!" Then how they all scoffed and sneered at him! (Matthew 9:23-24 TLB)

Now that seems very insensitive for the Good Shepherd. He goes to a funeral and tells everybody to get out, even in the middle of their mourning over this girl! What kind of man is this?

When the crowd was finally outside, Jesus went in where the little girl was lying and took her by the hand, and she jumped up and was all right again! The report of this wonderful miracle swept the entire countryside (Matthew 9:25-26 TLB).

Jesus Christ was a supernatural kind of man, a man who lived in a body, but nevertheless walked in the Spirit, not the flesh. He was a man who brought a new kind of authority into any room He entered.

Winter Sports and Switch-Hitters

In the Book of First Chronicles, an unusual brand of man surfaces that defies modern stereotypes. These individuals were known collectively as "David's mighty men." One of them named Jashobeam "...lifted up his spear against three hundred whom he killed at one time" (1 Chron. 11:11 NAS). Think of it: This one man single-handedly killed 300 armed opponents at one time! No, this isn't an Arnold Schwarzenegger script, this is historical fact.

Then there was Abshai. The Bible says, "As for Abshai the brother of Joab, he was chief of the thirty, and he swung his spear against three hundred and killed them; and he had a name as well as the thirty" (1 Chron. 11:20 NAS). I guess he did have a name.

Another man was into winter activities:

Benaiah...mighty in deeds, struck down the two sons of Ariel of Moab. He also went down and killed a lion inside a pit on a snowy day. And he killed an Egyptian, a man of great stature five cubits [seven-and-a-half feet] *tall. Now in the Egyptian's hand was a spear like a weaver's beam, but he went down to him with a club and snatched the spear from the Egyptian's hand, and killed him with his own spear* (1 Chronicles 11:22-23 NAS).

Now what kind of a guy was this? Do you ever feel like jumping into a pit with a lion? Maybe you do, but I've never acquired a taste for fighting lions on snowy days, especially in a pit. David had an entire army of men who commanded respect, even though they weren't passive enough to be "politically correct." The Bible says, "Now these are the ones who came to David at Ziklag…. They were equipped with bows, using both the right hand and the left to sling stones and to shoot arrows from the bow; they were Saul's kinsmen from Benjamin" (1 Chron. 12:1-2 NAS). Now these guys were the original "switch-hitters." This chapter describes even more incredible specimens of manhood:

> *And from the Gadites there came over to David in the stronghold in the wilderness, mighty men of valor, men trained for war, who could handle shield and spear, and whose faces were like the faces of lions, and they were as swift as the gazelles on the mountains. … These of the sons of Gad were captains of the army; he who was least was equal to a hundred and the greatest to a thousand* (1 Chronicles 12:8,14 NAS).

Can you imagine running into these dudes? Can you imagine facing a bunch of fighters whose wimpiest warrior was greater than a hundred normal soldiers? What if you drew the short straw and had to face some of the bigger and better bad boys, the soldiers who were equal to a thousand normal guys? I know what side I'd want to be on. I like those odds against an enemy. The fact is that within the Body of Christ we have some sons of God, great brothers and mighty men of valor, who are being trained for war. It is time for a Holy Ghost "attitude adjustment" concerning biblical manhood.

The *real* Jesus wasn't meek and mild in the effeminate way we understand these terms. Jesus was capable of some tough action and confrontational language. According to the home setting the Bible describes, Jesus would have had a lean body due to the disciplined life required by Joseph's carpentry trade. His muscles were strong from hard work. Jesus had to walk to the forest to harvest His own raw materials for His carpentry work. He had to cut trees down by hand with an axe, and He would have hand-carried those rough-hewn beams back home at nightfall. The years of rigorous self-dicipline on those long logging trips across rugged terrain, along with the grueling labor common to carpenters in that era, helped prepare Him for the 40-day fast He faced at the start of His adult ministry.

A Tough Day at the Temple

The 40-day fast described in the Gospels of Matthew, Mark, and Luke marked the beginning of Jesus' public ministry, and it was at this point that He began to exercise great authority (not passivity). His wilderness testing brought Him an inner fortitude that He would need to endure the hardship, fatigue, and opposition that lay ahead. It prepared Him for that day when He entered the Temple gate at Jerusalem with His disciples. I think the air was filled with the odors and noise of all the animals and humans pressed together by the crowd. Hard-faced priests and money changers were thrilled with their brisk business as they sat behind long tables. They were charging the highest prices they could squeeze from out-of-town Jews and local worshipers who arrived at the last minute to buy sacrificial animals or to change foreign currency into local currency.

And the Jews' passover was at hand, and Jesus went up to Jerusalem, and found in the temple those that sold

*oxen and sheep and doves, and the changers of money sit-
ting: and when He had made a scourge of small cords, He
drove them all out of the temple, and the sheep, and the
oxen; and poured out the changers' money, and over-
threw the tables; and said unto them that sold doves,
Take these things hence; make not My Father's house an
house of merchandise. And His disciples remembered that
it was written, The zeal of Thine house hath eaten Me up*
(John 2:13-17).

As Jesus took in this sordid picture of hypocritical
greed at the door of the Temple, His cheeks flushed. Quietly He braided together a whip of cords as His puzzled
disciples looked on. Suddenly, this powerfully built man
walked directly to the table where the fat money changers
sat. His calloused hands gripped the table laden with hundreds of pounds of coins and weights and hurled it vio-
lently across the court like it weighed nothing. Then He
struck the backs of the the cowering bankers, and they
scurried away in fear from the angry Rabbi.

Jesus and the "Laying On of Hands"

Even before the shocked crowd could comprehend
what was going on, Jesus charged on to the crowded
counters of the dove sellers and released the doves, ignoring the growing howl of protests swirling around Him.
Brushing aside the angry dealers in front of the cattle
pens, Jesus threw down the bars and drove the bellowing
animals out into the streets, then He turned on the dealers, delivering upon them the stinging blows of the whip
wielded in His work-hardened hands. He quickly cleared
the temple area of every buyer and seller, even though
coins still littered the Temple floor. His flying whip even
caught those who were illegally carrying jars and goods
through the Temple like it was a common roadway.

Finally, Jesus stood on the steps of the Temple flushed
and panting. In righteous anger, His eyes swept over the
crowd of faces still distorted by guilt and rage. Then He
removed every justification for their anger when He said,
"This is My authority. It is written, 'My Father's house
shall be called a house of prayer for all the nations,' but
you have made it a den of robbers. So go ahead—make My
day. Destroy this temple and in three days I will build it
back!" (the Dewey Freidel version of Matthew 21:13 and
John 2:19).

The "R-Rated" Redeemer

The "woe passages" Jesus gave us in chapter 23 of the
Book of Matthew sure don't sound like the typical positive
attitude messages we've come to expect. "You fools and
blind men... Woe to you, scribes and Pharisees, hypo-
crites!... Fill up then the measure of the guilt of your fathers. You serpents, you brood of vipers, how shall you
escape the sentence of hell?" (Mt. 23:17,29,32-33 NAS)
"Come on, Jesus. You're messing up our 'G' rating! We're
going to have to give this thing an 'R' for language and
violence!" No, it is time for us to grow up and discard our
one-sided plastic image of the Son of God.

Jesus was an outdoor man, He was a confrontational
man, and He was a courageous man. Pilate's words still
ring through the corridors of time, declaring something
to every generation that Pilate never intended: "Behold
the *man*!" (Jn. 19:5) Behold the man. Jesus Christ is the
Man to behold and imitate. How often do men in our day
perceive the Church of Jesus Christ as a feminine "bridle"
on their toughness? Over the centuries, the Church has
constantly lost men because it has primarily encouraged
men to pursue *feminine* virtues.

The Original "Tough" Love

We have failed to portray Christ the *man*, the strong, masculine confronter and protector that He was and is. We have failed to pursue masculine virtues in Christ-centered ways. It's not enough for Christians to portray a one-sided view of Jesus, and teach that weakness and tenderness are acceptable in a man. We must also portray the manly strength and moral firmness that is found in Him. In the men of this generation there is a hunger for a father. They hunger for masculine strength. The truth is that men can walk in the Lord's strength and personally display true toughness in the face of opposition. Decisiveness in the face of uncertainty is masculine. Saving power in the face of danger is masculine, and Jesus Christ set the mark we are to strive for.

What is the plight of the twentieth century male in America? Nobody likes to be called a "wimp," but this entire generation of males has been caricatured as wimps for half a century! Nearly 60 years ago, a man named Chick Young cashed in on the theme of the "poor husband" and launched the Sunday comic strip, "Blondie." His comic strip is still the most popular comic today, although it now competes with approximately 128 other comics in newspapers across America. Its central character, Dagwood, has been described as "a well-meaning idiot who is constantly outwitted by his children, his wife and his dog." Are there any "strong men" portrayed on television today? Yes, but these men are primarily bachelors, widowers, or divorcés. Married men are uniformly portrayed as somewhat ridiculous, incompetent, and perpetually confused.

Is Dad Bad?

What about movies? I thoroughly enjoy movies like *Dead Poet's Society*, but even this movie and others like it seem to have the subtle but dangerous subtheme that older men in authority are nearly always corrupt, that they thoroughly destroy and betray the idealism of the young! The bottom line of the message is simple: You cannot trust male authority. D.H. Lawrence once said, "Men have been depressed now for many years in their male and resplendent selves, depressed into dejection and almost abjection. Is that not evil?"

The typical father in America is enfeebled and rejected by his culture. He is represented on popular television programs as an object of suspicion, as a bad-tempered fool, or as a weak puddle of indecision. This can cause his sons to fall into secret despair because they desperately long for a manly model for their lives. By the time his sons are six years old, they will have adopted their mother's view of father, for good or for evil. By the time they are 20, they have adopted society's view of father. Since 1940, the mark of being a man has been to reject Dad! If you reject your father, then you are okay because you have paid the price of "being in."

Should Dagwood Join the Marines?

"Oh, it's just the old man. You know the old man doesn't know anything; he just doesn't know any better." You're probably not going to be offended by the twentieth century man because he's a wimp. He's always nice, and his modern beatitude is this: "Blessed are the passive for they shall avoid conflict." He's even worse than Dagwood because he'll never fully support his family or confront the forces that are trying to destroy it. While our society is turning out "Dagwoods" by the millions, God is calling this generation of men to be like Jesus in the Temple. We need to go to basic training for godly masculinity. Where have our passive men learned this passivity? It is primarily learned in the classrooms of our schools and churches!

When little Junior goes to school for the first time, he enters the classroom as a little boy (because that is what he is). He is naturally rambunctious. His voice is too shrill, so he suddenly receives his first lesson at school as confinements are placed upon him. (No, I am not against discipline or certain appropriate confinements.) On the first day of first grade, Junior wrestles on the playground and spits through the fence—and he promptly loses recess privileges. (Recess privileges are important to physically active young boys.) By the fourth grade, Junior has discovered that his body must remain quiet in class so he can win approval from adult female supervision. This way he can then escape in a world of fantasy during recess. So there he quietly sits, day after day, five days a week, nine months out of the year, under the feminine authority of a dedicated woman who quite naturally and innocently enforces schoolgirl rules.

Poppa Provides the Pattern

What do I mean by that? A female teacher keeps *maternal order* the way a woman would generally organize things. A man keeps *paternal order.* Jesus was raised under paternal order. Paul and Peter were raised under paternal order. That kind of training was also the norm in this country until the arrival of the industrial revolution. Although the mothers nurtured their sons in the early years, the fathers took over their instruction and became very close to their sons once they reached the age of six or seven. A boy learned the important female signals in his early years—from his time in the womb through those first years of critical bonding. But in the seventh year, the boy would enter a man's world.

Grandfather would teach him, tell him stories, and give him wisdom. His uncles would help mentor him, but his father would teach him a trade and model proper work habits and the ways of manhood before his eyes. His father, and other significant males in his life, gave him paternal order. He was often taught with an intimate, hands-on style, "Here son, I want to show you how to do this. Watch me. Now step over here and try to do it yourself, son."

Three Keys for Proper Passivity

What happens today? Every boy in school is taught traditional feminine etiquette and social values:

1. Talk only when asked to talk.
2. Do not initiate activity.
3. Don't try to supervise the activities of others.

So what is a boy supposed to do? The only place he can exert his masculinity is on the playground. He learns that inside the building, it is a woman's world, and outside is where he can still get away with being a man. That means that by the fourth grade, most boys have learned how to be passive because that is socially accepted in matriarchal society. I learned that very well.

I was the type of boy who gathered bumps and bruises like girls gather dolls, and I often came home with a bloody nose—usually with a smile on my face. I learned after a while that I was not going to be accepted that way at school. "You shouldn't fight on the playground. Just sit back. Always be quiet in class. Become like the teachers expect you to become: quiet and passive. You need to behave and learn just like the girls learn."

History doesn't agree with our modern foolishness. The educational process for girls in the past was quite different from the educational process for boys, and I'm not talking about providing second-class education for girls either. The education process should acknowledge the innate differences between males and females, including their differing strengths, weaknesses, and learning styles.

Waiting for the Recess Bell

In "modern" America, a man grows up and has a family, generally with a sadly predictable pattern. This man of the house probably won't speak unless someone asks him a direct question. His wife has now become the female figure modeled after the others who dominated him all those formative years in the classroom. The household environment becomes the school, and anywhere other than the house or the church represents "recess" for his masculinity. His wife gives the direction in the home and establishes the household environment, replacing the grade school teacher. Saddest of all, the man's children may now become his "classmates" in his marital classroom—the same classmates that he learned to avoid in the school system (he always got in trouble if he was caught talking to Johnny; he had to be quiet).

The office, the gym, or the lake may replace the playground in his mind. He gets involved and loses himself in his job because he doesn't want to go "inside." He wants to stay out at recess where he can be a man. When he does comes in, he obeys the rules ingrained in him. He quietly ignores the "classmates," or children, and he passively sits in front of the television with a six-pack, watching the game of the week.

Are We Damaged in Transit?

The American male enters the school system with great disadvantages. When a little boy starts school, he is less mature, and experts say he is underdeveloped compared to females his age with respect to vision, hearing, speech, writing skills, manual dexterity, and physical control. These are the same senses and physical capacities that are so vital to the learning process! Are boys brain-damaged? No, it is simply a difference in the development rates and makeup of boys and girls. The boys will eventually catch up. Countries who delay the beginning of formal schooling for children report substantially fewer learning disabilities and behavior problems, while their students hold their own academically with students who begin formal training at an earlier age.

As a result of this mismatch of delayed masculine development rates, little boy energy levels, and feminine order, a sad harvest of casualties has been produced. Let me list a few of them for you: Boys outnumber girls three to one in mental institutions for children. More than two out of three students who fail one or more grades are boys. Pathological conditions, including learning and behavioral disorders, are more common among males than among females of the same age at a ratio of ten to three. Among students who stutter, boys outnumber girls four to one, and three out of every four retarded readers are boys.

Making Do With Too Few

Are women to blame for this tragedy? Absolutely not! What does this have to do with our faith? Everything! Men are leaving churches in unprecedented numbers because they see it as a haven for feminine order. I'm not pointing my finger and saying anybody is wrong, but it is not balanced. Most of our Sunday schools are just like our public schools. They are operated under a female order, and the curriculum is written by dedicated females. Is it their fault? No, we have a serious shortage of men who are willing to provide paternal order.

There is nothing wrong with maternal instincts, or even the maternal way of dealing with boys. The problem is that there is a void where masculine paternal influence is concerned. Weldon Hardenbrook described the problem in his book, *Missing From Action*:

> "Remember more than 83 percent of all teachers in public elementary school are women. This works fine for girls who are ready to play school by participating in a feminine atmosphere. They sit quietly and listen to the teacher and take notes with their newly acquired skills in writing. Reading stories and gaining facts from books come easily for girls. They are usually eager to repeat the assignments that they have been asked to memorize.

> "Boys on the other hand, are quickly bored with this seemingly passive style of schooling. They have little interest in sitting still and being quiet. Reading and memorizing do not fit into the real world of young males. No matter how many words pass through the air, staying seated in one place for long periods of time does not connect with the natural processes by which boys learn. And most boys intuitively know it.

> "Those first years in elementary school come at a time when a boy is developing inherent masculine tendencies. He's shaping his skills for courage and strength. Thus he's constantly seeking action. While girls tend to want and think and feel, boys would rather see and do. They want to participate with vigorous verbal contact and aggressive physical action. When class ends the boys stampede the

playground to accomplish some small acts of bravery. If a girl joins them she's called a tomboy.

"Whether shooting at the air with gun bursts of imaginary bullets, hanging by the heels from playground bars, or simply shoving and pushing an opponent, boys will be and need to be boys. These very normal actions that boys display do not evoke the approval of the female-dominated system, even on the school playground. What is natural to young males is often viewed as bad behavior. Therefore many normal boys are labeled bad boys early in life when they're simply trying to discover their masculinity through innocent episodes of competitive game playing."

I received a note after preaching on manhood that I think is appropriate to pass along at this point:

"Pastor Dewey, this past week I participated in an intensive graduate course on the topic of classroom discipline in the public school. The three-credit course was taught by a female psychologist who used to be a school teacher. She spends several months on the road each year giving workshops to many public school systems. Of the 70 students in the course, only eight were men.

"Of the case studies looked at, almost all of them dealt with how to get boys from kindergarten through 12th grade to conform to class rules. Clearly boys were depicted as society's problem from childhood. The sad thing that struck some of the men was how scornfully this teacher spoke of her own family, calling her husband an 'angry fat lump,' and her 15-year-old son an 'unruly terror.' This woman, who is recognized as an expert in classroom discipline, has no respect for her family and probably feels no love from them. Her fake smile did not cover her sorrow."

"Nice Tank, Son"

Something is out of balance if we don't have male input, if the educational system itself is one-sided, and the boys are left hurting. How will we model Christian education? We must recognize the differences between boys and girls and learn how to properly channel the energy in little boys. My little boy was up at 6:15 one morning when I was studying the Word. He brought in his "G.I. Joe" army tank, and said, "Good morning, Dad. Watch this!" Then he launched a missile and it hit the side of the table. Now sometimes little boys need to be corrected and confined, yet they also need a channel for masculine expression and growth. I didn't yell, "Hey son, put that ungodly, violent stuff away!" Part of masculinity has to do with war—with the ability and the willingness to protect and shield others.

Read your Bible. David's mighty men of valor were warlike. They would jump in a pit to singlehandedly kill a lion! One guy would face 100 armed opponents. Another killed 300! Somebody had to teach them how to make war. These were tough dudes.

God Is Job Hunting

We need heroes today, and we need them desperately. If we don't have male heroes for our boys, if there are no mighty men of valor for them to imitate and look up to, then they will resort to worshiping and imitating whatever ungodly thing seems to have the most courage out in the world! The oldest book in the Bible, the Book of Job, describes a very wealthy man, who had all the marks of a man in boxer shorts. Drawing inspiration from Chapter 9 of Weldon M. Hardenbrook's excellent book *Missing From Action*, I want to paint a picture of a real man of God. If they had been available in his day, I believe Job would have been wearing boxer shorts—even in those rough days on the ash heap—because he was a real man. He was God's man, and he is still a hero for the Church today.

Number one: *Job had a sense of history*. Chapter 29 of the Book of Job reveals that this man was in touch with the past. If you don't know history, you will repeat history's mistakes needlessly. We need to know how God dealt with people in the past, and how men dealt with God.

I love to quote from Alfred Edersheim's detailed sketches of Jewish social life in the time of Jesus. I want to know how they trained their sons and daughters in those days. There is wisdom in the Word of God, and there is wisdom to be gleaned from history as well. Paul said, "...stand fast, and hold the traditions which ye have been taught..." (2 Thess. 2:15). What traditions have we passed down as fathers that our fathers before us learned from their fathers, traditions about training men for their godly masculine role in life? I think they are all but gone. Every man seems to be doing his own thing, and it looks like our heroes are those slouches on television. If that is true, then we're in deep trouble. Unlike most "modern" men, Job had a sense of history.

Number two: *Job was close to his children*. He was vitally interested in meeting both their physical and spiritual needs. The Bible says Job rose early to offer burnt offerings for them (Job 1:5). His children were a prime source of Job's pleasure. What are the prime sources of your pleasure? Many dads are running from their children!

They are uncomfortable with them, so they get lost on the golf course, at work, or in front of the television. Many of us are afraid of our kids. In contrast, Job made his children a primary source of his earthly pleasure.

Number three: *Job was a father to orphans.* (See Job 29:12.) This man knew how to help others. He was a hero to the hurting. I grew up in a lower-middle-class family where money was often scarce, but I still remember how my dad would gather together money, goods, food, and clothing to give to somebody else in need. I didn't think anything of it at the time, but now I remember that and think, "What a man!" What a man. That was his movie money and his milkshake money in the tight days. Sometimes it was tough for us just to go to the Tastee Freeze to order a 35-cent milkshake. My father's example made an impression on me. I knew he was doing something that was godly and right when I saw him take out of his own and give to others in need. Job was that kind of man. He was a father to the fatherless.

The Church will become what it is destined to be only when the men in the Church are willing to become fathers to the fatherless. If we don't provide father images for them, they will go out among their peers and try to mentor one another in the artificial family life of street gangs. It takes godly men to father the fatherless.

Number four: *Job was a champion of justice.* Job didn't live on an ash heap all of the time; that was just a brief phase of his life. He was incredibly aggressive where injustice was concerned! He said, "I broke the fangs of the wicked, and snatched the victims from their teeth" (Job 29:17 NIV). This was some man. It appears that Job knew how to handle himself, and he had learned how to discipline his enemies! Why do men leave movie rental stores with stacks of movies featuring strong heros who always make the "bad guys" wish they'd stayed home and left the helpless alone?

Why do men like to watch John Wayne, Clint Eastwood, Arnold Schwarzenegger, Steven Segal, and countless other hero types who deal ruthlessly with evildoers? God has put within us something that wants to punish injustice. We want to destroy any enemy who dares to mess up people's lives! I'm not advocating all the ways these Hollywood heroes use to get the job done, but I'm saying it rings a bell in men because God made them that way!

Men should not feel guilty over something that is innately masculine. Real men get angry over injustice. Job got angry when people harassed widows or orphans. He let everyone know he was coming after them if they violated the innocent. God has placed that same protecting spirit in us! A real man isn't happy until he is able to protect. I believe America is wanting to see real men rise up. The real man of God hitches up his boxer shorts and gets busy enforcing justice.

Number five: *Job was merciful.* This man of God was balanced in his strength. He could move in both the compassion and the strength of God. John Templeton, a strong believer and a billionaire, as a matter of conviction, has given millions of dollars away to thousands of needy people. Job was that kind of man. He was a living, God-powered mercy machine in boxer shorts (figuratively speaking); and God used him greatly. Real men flex more than their muscles; they stretch their hearts and reach out in mercy to the hurting, the repentant, and the needy.

Number six: *Job earned respect.* He didn't demand it, he *earned* it. Job received respect because he freely demonstrated the mercy of God to others, and he fairly administrated the strength and justice of God. He was a man who fearlessly defended the helpless and challenged the lawless. You couldn't pussyfoot around with him; unlike other men of lesser character, this man meant what he said. What about you? Are your boxer shorts on straight? Do you mean the things you say? How far will you go to honor your promises?

Number seven: *Job had a life of consistency.* One out of every four Americans will move this year. I'm surprised that furniture manufacturers haven't installed wheels as standard equipment on all of their products. We live in temporary neighborhoods, and we've become "the land of strangers." It may still be a beautiful day in Mr. Roger's neighborhood, but if anybody's home, he probably couldn't tell you his neighbor's name. If we get somebody else's mail by mistake, it's a hopeless task to deliver it ourselves! Most of us don't know anybody on our street anymore because everybody is playing musical houses. The restless male is at it again.

Men are trying to find themselves. They are "father hungry," and they don't know who they are. Many are going out to make more money, but their frantic search is ruining the security of their families. Job said, "I'm staying in this place, and I'm going to make a witness here for the Kingdom of God, come hell or high water. I'm not going to greener pastures somewhere else; I'm going to make it here because God called me here." How do you know where God calls you? It is usually where you are, that's it. You don't have to pray and fast for 40 days; God puts you where He wants you, and He'll move you if and when He is ready. Just stay put and do His bidding.

Number eight: *Job was wise.* God called Job a perfect man because he pursued the Lord (see Job 1:8). Most men today have been taught that the pursuit of God is basically feminine. I thank God for women who have pursued the

Lord, including the company of women who followed Jesus on the earth. However, Jesus also had His bold men. We need to pursue God and allow Him to train us to be like David's mighty men of valor. We are to become trained men of war with faces like lions and legs as swift as gazelles. We have to transfer this physical description to the spirit, and say, "Lord Jesus, teach us to rise up as men. Heal our souls and help us to become a mighty fortress of wisdom and strength standing against injustice." God will bless the Church if we heed Him; then there will be a balance between feminine godliness and masculine fortitude while both work together in completion. Jesus, the man of God, yielded to the zeal of God and used a whip as well as the cross to fulfill the will of the Father. May we walk in the fullness of manhood as God the Father has always intended.

Chapter 7

Real Dads
Wear Boxer Shorts

Behold, I will send you Elijah the prophet before the coming of the great and dreadful day of the Lord: and he shall turn the heart of the fathers to the children, and the heart of the children to their fathers, lest I come and smite the earth with a curse (Malachi 4:5-6).

The typical man is taking a pretty hard hit in the movies, popular sitcoms, and the music world. Most modern males don't know who they are, and many pretend to be macho to hide their sense of rejection and low self-esteem. Our society has skillfully trained us to be passive eunuchs when it comes to leadership, but God wants us to break out of that mold! God needs some real soldiers in this hour, and I believe He is going to have them.

Malachi was the last prophet to hear from God and proclaim His Word to Israel in the Old Testament. Malachi's last words of prophecy sealed the Old Covenant and marked the beginning of 400 years of silence, when

God's voice was not heard in Israel. Only with the emergence of John the Baptist from the wilderness was the silence broken with the prophetic announcement that the Kingdom of God was coming. Look closely at Malachi's final words: "And he shall turn the heart of the fathers to the children, and the heart of the children to their fathers..." (Mal. 4:6).

Paternal Prophecy

I want you to notice that this prophecy is *paternal*. God is prophesying through Malachi that He is going to do something with *fathers*. Is this just "another example" of the Bible's male chauvinistic prophetic language? Does this prophecy mean that God isn't really interested in women? No! God is interested in both parts of the unique race He created in His image. However, He speaks to those members of the race who are in the greatest danger of abdicating the positions He has assigned to them. God does not want men to abdicate their God-given role as directors and leaders. He declares prophetically that He will restore the hearts of the fathers to the children, and the hearts of the children to their fathers.

The majority of America's children today are being taught by the media and by society in general to hate their fathers. The mark of a "man" in society is not that he has experienced his bar mitzvah, or that he has learned and recited God's Holy Word. In fact, there isn't any kind of special rite for a boy who is entering manhood today other than his willful rejection of his father's authority and position as head of the family.

God is out to clean up that mess. He puts a "stinger" on His declaration that most people don't like to quote: "And he shall turn the heart of the fathers to the children, and the heart of the children to their fathers, *lest I come and smite the earth with a curse*" (Mal. 4:6). We need to co-operate with God's Spirit so that our land will not be struck with a curse! We have time because God has warned us in advance. God is on the scene. He is doing things in every field, and He is saying, "I want men to stand in this hour, and if they'll stand, then I will heal them."

God wants to heal us in the depths of our souls, and He wants to teach us, once again, what it is to be whole in Him. As He speaks to our hearts individually, He is also gathering men and fathers together. He wants us to find one another, for then we will find ourselves working in our society, moving this nation toward the restoration that God said would take place in the last days. Remember that none of this will "just happen" by itself. It will only happen as we cooperate with God's Word.

It's Up to You, Dad

You have a part to play in the prophetic fulfillment of Malachi 4:6. How important is it? It is very important because you're a part of it. Experts agree that the major problems troubling America, including the rising rates of juvenile delinquency, violent crime, suicide, and illegitimate births, are all rooted in fathers who have turned their hearts from their children!

I declare to you that the Word of the Lord to every male is that you are called to be a *spiritual father*! That includes single males and childless husbands. God has called us all to be spiritual fathers. We are to be mentors who will pay the price and make the commitment to lead other men into the truths of Jesus Christ.

Single males are the greatest exploiters of American women today because they have abdicated their true roles as protectors and shields. These men have become "entre-preneurs of pleasure" who take advantage of lonely women on a massive scale. Single women, especially young women who no longer enjoy the covering and pro-tection of their fathers, are so lonely and hungry for love and affirmation that they often dismiss their inner misgiv-ings to meet every lustful desire of these hedonistic entre-preneurs of pleasure.

"Throwaway" Fatherhood

Unfortunately, there is no commitment or covenant in this picture of "pleasure." When such men are finished and their lusts are temporarily satisfied, they will dispose of such women in the same way they dispose of any other "product" they use. Outside of covenant, female sexual function just becomes another "commodity" in this "me-oriented" consumer society. Once a woman is used, once the package is opened, she can be thrown away or put on a shelf with the other "trophies" until lust hits again. These men may make "promises," if necessary, to get what they want for the moment, but they will never *commit.*

The sexual entrepreneur is especially attracted by the vulnerability of single women who have been left un-protected by absentee fathers or very passive fathers. Why? Their hurt makes them "easy prey." We are pay-ing for it dearly in this country. Sex has now become a cas-ual recreational activity totally divorced from covenantal commitment—"After all, it's free and natural, isn't it?"

Sex is designed for pleasure and "recreation," but only within the safe harbor of lifelong commitment and total covenant. Today, our society has rejected God and the foundations of social order He established. It makes the life of open fornication and adultery look nice and cute, while anyone who believes and proclaims the standards of God's Word is ridiculed as an outdated prude who is stuck in the repressive standards of the Victorian era. When someone accuses, "You must be Victorian if you believe that kind of stuff!" I just answer, "Hey, the truths I believe date *way* back, even earlier than the Victorian era. In fact, the truth about sex goes all the way back to the heart of God Himself! He says, 'I've got a way for you to live because I have created you. Recreational sex will destroy you.' "

Morons for Christ?

How long will it take for us to get the message? Our race is ravaged by all kinds of deadly new strains of venereal disease, but we still think we can play around. While statistics clearly show how the cases of death and sickness due to STD's have risen astronomically, we still hear television pundits like Mr. Donahue saying to the Christian, "Get back in your corner and shut up. Keep your judgmental narrow-thinking mind to yourself." Our well-dressed television talk show hosts love to call those who talk about Jesus "morons," while others parade before the public in open sin and lewdness, receiving the full blessing and approval of these hosts of harlotry.

One of the topics you are unlikely to see on *Donahue*, or any other secular talk show, is how much it costs us to underwrite this "free life style of recreational sex" in America. You and I have to help pick up the tab for uncovenanted sex to the tune of $20 billion a year! This is how much it costs annually to care for single mothers and the unwanted children left behind "the boys who call themselves men." These little boys in grown bodies think they're studs. They are driven by their hormones and are empowered by our nation's godless humanistic philosophy to take advantage of every lonely woman they can find and seduce!

"Hi, I'm an Unnecessary Mutation"

Our society has been structured to create a passive male. Weldon Hardenbrook has some serious quotes from today's women. First is one from Margaret Mead, a leading anthropologist, and a powerful influence for modern women. Consider what she has to say about the male's role in society: "Man is uncertain, undefined, and perhaps unnecessary." That makes you feel good, doesn't it? A lot of women have also read the works of the feminist theorist Elizabeth Davis. Carefully read what she has to say about men in society and the family:

> "Maleness remains a recessive genetic trait like color blindness and hemophilia, with which it is linked. The suspicion that maleness is abnormal and that the white chromosome is an accidental mutation boding no good for the race, is strongly supported by the recent discovery by geneticists that congenital killers and criminals are possessed of not one, but two Y-chromosomes, bearing a double dose as it were of genetically undesirable maleness."

So maleness is what? It is "undesirable." It is an "accidental mutation," and it's not good for the human race. That really does something for the male's inferiority complex, doesn't it? It is not enough that all of the television shows make fun of Dad, or put the male in a bad light. As a matter of fact, it is even creeping into the Church accidentally. Ronda told me that a number of the skits for our church's Vacation Bible School portrayed men as "dodo's," while the women were always the saviors who came in with the answer! Now you can only take so much of that over a 10- or 15-year period before you begin to really be-lieve it!

I'm not saying that women never have the answers, but they don't have them all the time! Now leave us a little dig-nity! I'm here to proclaim that when Pilate said, "Behold the man," he didn't know just how true his words were! Behold the man! Jesus Christ is our model.

Did you know that Jesus was not only a Son, but He is also a father? "Now hold on. Jesus is the Son, and He is part of the Trinity. It's God the Father, God the Son, and God the Holy Spirit. So what are you doing? What are you breaking up the Trinity for? Jesus isn't the Father." No, Je-sus is not the Father in the Trinity, but He is a father in re-lationship to His Church. He is the father of the New Covenant. Jesus has a dual role as both father and hus-band of His Bride, the Church. According to Isaiah's ever-lasting prophecy, the Messiah is "...The mighty God, The everlasting Father, The Prince of Peace" (Is. 9:6). He was talking about Jesus Christ, the Messiah who was to come. Jesus brings men into fatherhood. He helps us under-stand the masculine nature of God.

Frankly, I don't care what the twentieth century's phi-losophers and leaders are saying about it; it's not working anyhow. When are we going to come to our senses and recognize the obvious fact that the Word of God is truth? God didn't give us His Word just so a bunch of Christians could walk around proclaiming the "last days" with signs saying, "This is the way, walk ye in it." God's Word is true, whether you have the signs out there or not. God says we are to follow His Word because it will bring us life.

Real Men Mentor

The truth is that *real men* don't just make babies;they care for every child they sire, and they also cover and shel-ter the babies deserted by others. This is the masculine spirit of the everlasting Father! Jesus Christ is a father to the fatherless, so what does this have to do with us? I believe it has everything to do with us. I believe the restored Church will be a community of fathers and mentors! This community of true fathers will take their calling and assignment seriously.

Several years ago, God gave me a dream that helped me understand and clarify the vision He gave me for fatherhood in the Church. In the dream, I saw a young Black man fall dead in a shoot-out. He appeared to have been in his early 20's. I also saw a Black teenager, who was about 13 years old, watching. I had no doubt that this young teenager had idolized the older Black man who had been shot. Again, this is a picture of America. When a father is absent, the older children will try to father the younger ones, and it doesn't work.

For a brief moment in the dream, the spirit of the man who had been shot came back to life and left the prone body. It stood up and told the 13-year-old boy, "Don't walk in my footsteps because this is where it leads." Then the man's spirit went back into his body to lie in death. But just before it returned to the body, I felt like the man also put this young Black teenage boy into my hands and said, "Here." I knew that God was confirming to me through that dream that the men in His Church were to be fathers to the fatherless.

Monuments Are "Out"

Christians should always remember that when they talk about facilities, activities in a community, or recreational playgrounds, we're talking about meeting people where they live and hurt. When we talk about a life style and everything necessary to facilitate that life style of supply instead of want, we need to remember that we're talking about people whom God loves. What we are *not* talking about is some kind of "feel good" project that will allow us to have our pictures taken (using a wide lens to accommodate our egos) as memorials to our accomplishments. Facilities, buildings, and programs exist solely to fulfill the purposes of God in the lives of people. They provide places for fellowship, worship, teaching, training, and recreation. They are tools to help men in the church develop relationships with fatherless young people so they don't follow the way of the man who died in the dream.

Where did fatherhood come from? What is it? The essence of fatherhood is best described by one word, a word that has been under great attack. Enemies have fought to annihilate this word, and it has been relegated to the dead civilizations of antiquity. This important word is *patriarchy*, a Greek compound word consisting of *patria*, which means "father or family," and *archy*, means "beginning, first in origin, first to rule." A patriarch is a family ruler. God is calling us to have multiple generations of families in the Lord. The Old Covenant speaks of Abraham, Isaac, Jacob, and all their offspring.

Today, we often see God move in the lives of one generation in a church, but any kind of moral failure or split can cause the local church to fall to pieces. That is not God's plan. He says that if men will stand and come together, then He will invest His power, His glory, and His masculine spirit in them. He will make them a generation that will produce another like it, and another and another!

God Bless This Mess

The problem is that we're always trying to "get out of this mess," aren't we? We say, "Well, God's not really interested in bringing you into a very definite, specific, detailed walk because Jesus is coming soon!" I hope He does, but a lot of people have said that for the last 200 to 300 years. Maybe what God is saying to us is, "Why don't you quit looking up there at the sky so much, and get to work in My service down here. Haven't I already commanded you, 'Go ye therefore, and teach [disciple] all nations...'? (Mt. 28:19). I will take care of splitting the sky wide open and coming back to get you."

God also gave us a little clue. He is not coming back to get us until the restoration of all things that the prophets have spoken, and until His Bride is spotless and without wrinkle (see Acts 3:21; Eph. 5:27). His Bride won't be ready until men get prepared and learn how to wield the sword, protect their families, and train up a generation that is taught the Word of God—that is *patriarchy*. What causes spots on a wedding dress? Being in the wrong places. What causes wrinkles? Sitting down! It's time for men to get into the right place and stand so the wrinkles in the Bride's gown will fall out.

Jesus said something about patriarchy that reveals His supreme mission on earth! Jesus said, "I am the way, the truth, and the life: no man cometh unto the Father, but by Me" (Jn. 14:6). Many Christians, and even ministers of the gospel, like to *partially* quote this Scripture: "I am the way, the truth, and life." And that's it, they stop right there. Look again. Jesus didn't stop there. He said something else that reveals the deeper purpose of God. He also said, "...no man cometh unto the Father, but by Me" (Jn. 14:6). This is His supreme mission: Jesus wants to get you to the Father.

When Jesus had to make a radical departure from the era of past tradition, He always did it. Jesus chose 12 men because of patriarchy, so the fathers would be the leaders of their homes and the new Church. Now God is not squashing or quenching women. He's saying, "In My Church, there are many varieties of ministries and gifts, and women are to flow in those." However, He has ordered that as far as direction and government go, it will follow patriarchal order; it is manly, and it follows the masculine spirit of God.

> *Philip said to Him, "Lord, show us the Father, and it is enough for us." Jesus said to him, "Have I been so long with you, and yet you have not come to know Me, Philip? He who has seen Me has seen the Father; how do you say, 'Show us the Father'? Do you not believe that I am in the Father, and the Father is in Me? The words that I say to you I do not speak on My own initiative, but the Father abiding in Me does His works"* (John 14:8-10 NAS).

The eternal plan of God is not going to be changed, no matter how "enlightened" or "new" our humanist philosophy pretends to be. Most of our "modern" thinking is anti-family, and it is rooted in blatant self-indulgence. It all spells destruction for women, for boys, and for girls. American men have left the Father and the Church. Because they abdicated their role, we are in bondage to an educational process that doesn't even understand us. Nevertheless, the trumpet of God's authority rings out to call us to an obedience which, in turn, will bring us into security, freedom, power, and glory. God's headship and masculine authority bring accountability when we say "Yes."

It's Time for a Head Count

Any man who wants to be the "head" of his household must ask himself, "How do I handle that headship? Who is my head? Who am I accountable to?" Scripture says, "Obey your leaders, and submit to them; for they keep watch over your souls, as those who will give an account..." (Heb. 13:17 NAS). Now that authority can be abused, but just because a person or group abuses authority and headship does not mean that we turn from it to our own destruction. We have to say, "God, here's Your ideal. How then should we handle this problem?"

Women feel secure when they know they have a court of appeal, when they know that their husband or father doesn't just rule them with a rod of iron, but rules out of the love of Christ and that he is accountable to other men. Colonial America was run according to a biblical structure in every community. I remember reading that, in one Pennsylvania county, there was a case where a husband refused to engage in intercourse with his wife for two years. She got frustrated and went to the elders of the local church. Although her husband was warned, he did nothing, so he was excommunicated from the church.

We say, "Well, big deal, he was excommunicated." It doesn't mean that much to us today, but back then there was only one church. If you had committed adultery or failed to be a good father, then you repented and made restitution, or you would be excommunicated and banned from the Table of the Lord.

Once we come to the real God-man of the universe, He initiates a whole new life style for us based on *agape* love. It requires us to be men, *real men* who aren't afraid to wear boxer shorts. Now how do we practice that? Let me give you some quick pointers:

Number one: *Husbands, love your wives just as Christ also loved the Church.* What is so masculine about that? I'm glad that I never wake up and hear Jesus saying, "I don't feel like loving you today. I don't feel like protecting you today. I don't feel like honoring My Word in your life today. I don't feel covenanted to you today, so you go out there on your own and try to make it." You know what would happen to me? The same thing that would happen to you. God isn't like man that He should lie (see Num 23:19). Do

I deserve that grace every day? No, but He covers me in His grace moment by moment because He is consistent in His love and commitment to His covenant. You and I are to have that same kind of contract in our homes. There may be days when I don't feel it, but I refuse to renege on my covenant commitment. I'm in this thing for life. Real men don't tell their wives to get lost or trade them in for a newer model.

Number two: *Love commits.* How do we know that? Masculine love bears all things. We don't like this talk to-day because then we can't say, "I can't stand it anymore. I have to see a lawyer because we're having trouble in our marriage." *Commitment* is the cure, not resentment and at-torney's fees. According to First Corinthians 13, love com-mits because it bears all things.

Number three: *Love sacrifices.* We really hate the "s" word. "Pastor, do you mean I just can't come in here any-time I want, raise my hands, and say, 'Oh isn't this won-derful?' and then go live like hell?" That's right. "But don't twentieth-century men get what they want when they want it?" No, we have a heart problem that desperately needs to be healed. Most of us have been separated from our earthly fathers, the men who were designated to bring us into a model relationship with our heavenly Father. It is God's plan for sons to see in their daddies' love a shadow of His ultimate fatherly love in Heaven.

Now we've been separated and estranged from our earthly daddies, and we hardly know them. We grew up too quickly, and dad was always at the office, or at the fac-tory, or at the school. We spent very little time together. God says the Christian community has to change that. Man of God, you have to find ways to work with your sons. Bring them into your workplace and give them a "show and tell" experience if you have to. Single men, don't hang your heads and say, "Well, right now I don't have any children." You have plenty of children. Just look around.

I've lost count of the guys who have asked me to "hold them accountable." They're searching for the father they never had. I say, "God, I can't. I can't take them all!" I'm talking about men in their 20's and 30's too. They're saying, "I need somebody. I'll get in trouble if I'm not answering to somebody." There are young men in every church and community who desperately need a spiritual father who will commit to mentor them.

Number four: *Love fights.* It is a shame that the masculine role of God has been diluted and watered down. I'm not saying the Christian man needs to go get a sword and chop somebody's head off. Rather, I'm echoing the apostle Paul: "Fight the good fight of faith" (1 Tim. 6:12a NAS). The Bible is a violent book, and much of the violence is sanctioned by God when the power is given to the state to keep peace. God's people are to function in justice and peace. Jesus was violent in the Temple, and probably the ultimate act of violence is everlasting punishment in hell for those who chose to lose. Love fights. Learn to fight evil like men. Come out of your passive ways, learn to stand your ground, learn to confront evil.

Number five: *A godly, manly love pursues virtue.* The Latin word *vir* means "a man." *Virtus* means "moral perfection," so virtue links masculinity with moral excellence. We have sure wandered away from that meaning. Real masculinity brings moral excellence onto the scene. God has called us to be tough men who can resist evil, flee from lust, and pursue virtue.

Number six: *Real men are gentle.* Do you know what *gentle* really means? It originates from a Latin term meaning "clan, or belonging to the same family." So the term *gentleman* properly refers to a family man, or a man of the clan. I get weary of hearing about playboys and "Don Juans" considered to be Mr. Erudite Gentleman. They are not gentlemen; they are just a bunch of immature jerks running around looking for something they lost or never had. A real gentleman is a family man.

Number seven: *Real men are men of comradeship.* Jesus regularly pulled Peter, James, and John aside to talk to them and share a rich, male relationship with them. He had women friends as well, and He had women who followed Him. He greatly valued these women of faith, and many of their dialogues have been recorded in the Scriptures. However, Jesus demonstrated the importance of being with other men. Wives need to understand that it is important for a husband to spend an occasional "night out with the guys," just as it is important for wives to spend time with other women. Men need "male talk" in the same way women need "female talk."

Number eight: *Real men initiate.* The love of God the Father is a masculine love that initiates. Jesus openly showed us His love for His Father. He referred to His Father by using the most intimate of words—the early Bible translators were even ashamed to translate it's true meaning! Its true Aramaic meaning is "daddy," not father. Jesus knew Daddy was with Him. That transcends everything. Don't be afraid to initiate things with your sons and daughters. Boldly express and demonstrate your love and commitment to your family as only a real man can. (And don't forget your boxer shorts.)

Chapter 8

How to Raise Kids While Wearing...

It is rare today to see a preteen who shows the basic gift of childhood. What have they lost? They have lost the basic gifts of innocence and play. These two things go together. Only children really know how to play and run and frolic. I think it is interesting that Jesus rebuked His disciples for getting after a group of children who wanted to see Him. "But Jesus called them unto Him, and said, Suffer little children to come unto Me, and forbid them not: for of such is the kingdom of God" (Lk. 18:16). Jesus actually became indignant because the disciples were rebuking the little children!

Admit It, Kid

There is something wonderful about being childlike. A few years ago, I escaped from a boring "adult thing" and joined the kids out in the yard. I had a great time running around trying to catch lightning bugs with my son. When was the last time you tried to do that? It's fun. Go ahead, admit it: You still have that child in you. Let him loose once in a while and have a good time.

Faith and discipleship should work hand-in-hand with childlikeness, although most of us act like they are "mutually exclusive." My three-year-old son, Isaac, was really getting frustrated that night in the yard because for some reason the lightning bugs were flying too high for him to reach. Then I heard him run by me and say, "I'm going to have to pray in the name of Jesus for this bug!" I thought, *My goodness, this is real. It's operative in his little spirit. He's been trained in the church and by Mommy and Daddy, but Isaac's childlikeness believes that in every situation he is in, the name of Jesus is going to make a difference.*

Dads can learn from their children—if they have a childlike spirit. I was sitting in the kitchen when Ronda tried 15 times to get the microwave to work. So what did "Mr. Mechanic" do? I thought of Isaac. Then I said, "In the name of Jesus, microwave start!" Ronda looked at me with an odd expression, but suddenly that microwave started up! The Lord wants men to be childlike. The problem is that our society is always trying to squeeze us into its own mold, and that mold has an especially ungodly effect on our childhood.

"Kids Are Too Childish"

Society isn't happy with kids being kids. Parents jump on the bandwagon and get their kids too wired up and too tight. God says we are to let the children be children. We've "professionalized" our children too early. Major cosmetic companies like Max Factor, Revlon, and Clairol are all targeting new products like makeup and "beauty care treatments" toward nine-year-old girls! No, I'm not talking about playing with lipstick and fake fingernails. This is the real stuff, complete with the thought that they are incomplete without the "help" of these products! Satan wants to kill this generation of children. If he can't do it through abortion, then he will try to do it by making them miss their childhood.

By the time a girl reaches her fifteenth birthday, she will probably be wearing more nail enamel, eye shadow, blush, and foundation than any other demographic group of women in the United States. A French company even came out with a $25-an-ounce perfume for girls! Who are the targets? This perfume is aimed at girls between the ages of 9 and 14 years old. Enough is enough! We're treating children like they are adults way too early! We're bringing them in on major family decisions and issues—along with the tremendous pressures they create. We treat them as partners, and sometimes the children are even used as therapists to their unsettled parents.

God has already spoken on the subject: "Unless the Lord builds the house, they labor in vain who build it..." (Ps. 127:1 NAS). There is both labor and responsibility involved in parenting, but it is even more important to realize that only God can really build the family unit. We have to remember that we are different from the society around us, and we can't let it squeeze us into its mold. The problem is, most Christian men don't care. Then we get frustrated because we have never given our families over to the Lord Jesus Christ.

"I Am Not God"

The most important attitude adjustment you can make is to say out loud to yourself: "I am not God, and I can't be God." You need to be thankful for that. That means you will not be perfect in the way you parent. However, if you give your children to the Lord, then you can share the responsibility of training, leading, and caring for them with Someone who is perfect. Your children ultimately belong to God, not you.

Our information-rich society has produced "panic-stricken" parents who are paralyzed from an information overload. They fear that if they do something wrong, they may permanently damage the psyche of their child! They fear their little six-year-old may not grow up to be normal just because they didn't do all the things a particular school of thought is saying should be done. No, we can't measure our parenting success by the ever-changing opinions of a school of thought, a social scientist, or the denizens of child psychologists who were spawned in the 1960's and 70's. The question is this: *What does the Word of God say?*

"Unless the Lord builds the house, they labor in vain who build it..." (Ps. 127:1 NAS). So what should a good Christian father in manly boxer shorts do about his children?

Number one: *Pray.* Pray for your children on your own, and pray in agreement with your spouse. Pray about the influence of friends and media on your children. This releases the power of God, which will bind every evil principality that would put your children in a mold too early. Current children's television shows can make a discerning parent sick to his stomach with their "politically correct" and "fashionably correct" messages. The children on screen have all the right name tags on their clothing, and their animated facial expressions, conversations, and sexual innuendos are coached to match the adult life styles they are emulating. Little kids even have dance parties just like the teenagers.

If you haven't noticed, the world wants us to think that the innocent days are over when girls dress up like Mommy and look ridiculous with big high heels and purses. Today's society says our little girls have to be very mysterious, and that they should already be displaying a well-developed "feminine mystique" (sexual attraction). No, we don't have to buy the lie. If we really want the Lord to build our house, then we have to pray. Pray for your little one's friends, and begin to pray now for the friends that will come along in the future! Begin to pray for their future mates *right now*! "Dear Lord, they're alive right now. We pray that Your angels would be dispatched to protect them and watch over them. May they grow up in the fear and admonition of Your Word!" Isn't that worth a prayer, starting now? Why wait until they are 21 or 22? Start praying now.

Is It Time to Change Yet?

Pray about the influence of the mass media over our children. I believe that most Americans really want to do what is right. One sexual survey reported that most Americans still believe that premarital sex is wrong, and most say that running around in an adulterous affair is wrong. Most of those polled also believed that homosexuality is wrong. The media would like us to believe that everybody has changed, even though it isn't true. And as a result, some people change just because they think everybody else is. There is still a very strong Judeo-Christian ethic in the foundation of this country.

Number two: *Read the Word of God.* If we don't read God's Word, then we are doomed to "parent by trends." Child abuse is a terrible thing, but on the other hand, there is also an abuse of *not* using the rod of correction. That is abusing your child too! "Do you mean you believe in spanking, Pastor Dewey? Why that's archaic! That's violent!" Who says? Was it some fiddler on the roof with

14 rebellious kids running around snorting coke and ped-dling drugs? We must not let the world tell us how we're to keep house.

Seat-of-the-Pants Discipline

I'm amazed when I hear Christian adults say, "I'm barely able to control my children. I can't do a thing with them." Well, get the rod out. It is there specifically so you can apply a little protoplasmic posterior stimulation to the seat of correction. It helps. No, I'm not talking about child abuse: No parent is authorized to beat a child. I'm talking about adult authority. Every child needs and longs for authority in his life. Children want to know that some-body is in charge because it provides security and reassur-ance that somebody cares enough to correct them.

We need to read what the Word of God says so we are not doomed to parent according to the fickle trends of so-ciety. Contrary to popular claims, do you realize that there is no evidence proving that academic preschool will prepare your child for Harvard, or that children who read by the age of three will be geniuses in high school? In fact, there isn't any proof that my child needs to be bi-lingual by the time he's six, or that he should know how to backstroke like Olympic gold medal winners, and play T-ball at age five to make it to the New York Mets as an adult. Man of God, hitch up your shorts and put a stop to the stupidity. Don't let anybody rob your children of their childhood!

Number three: *Let the children play.* God wants us to preserve the childlike spirits He implanted in our chil-dren. Let them play!

Thus saith the Lord of hosts; I was jealous for Zion with great jealousy, and I was jealous for her with great fury.

Thus saith the Lord; I am returned unto Zion, and will dwell in the midst of Jerusalem: and Jerusalem shall be called a city of truth; and the mountain of the Lord of hosts the holy mountain. Thus saith the Lord of hosts; There shall yet old men and old women dwell in the streets of Jerusalem, and every man with his staff in his hand for very age. And the streets of the city shall be full of boys and girls playing in the streets thereof (Zechariah 8:2-5).

Kids on Every Street!

We are in the middle of a revival, or restoration, right now. The Bible says, "And that He may send Jesus, the Christ appointed for you, whom heaven must receive until the period of restoration of all things about which God spoke by the mouth of His holy prophets from ancient time" (Acts 3:20-21 NAS). We're in the midst of this restoration now, and it will just grow in its degree until even the elderly in New York City will once again be able to sit on a park bench without worrying about muggers or robbers. The prophet also prophesied that the city will be filled with boys and girls playing in its streets. God portrays His restored Kingdom as filled with playing children. He couldn't be any clearer than this!

When I was a kid, my family used to have a blast every Sunday afternoon when we left church. We would change our clothes, then go over to Grandmom's house for a great meal. Best of all, everybody expected the kids to be kids. While the adults ate, talked, or snored all afternoon, we played ourselves into a frenzy until sunset. Then we collapsed in our parents' car. We were children, and we were allowed to be children.

Many dads are apprehensive about their children's "careers." They complain, "We're afraid our kids will never make it." Never make what? Let God give them their calls. Let God be the one who says there's a special gift in here. "Behold, children are a gift of the Lord; the fruit of the womb is a reward. Like arrows in the hand of a warrior, so are the children of one's youth" (Ps. 127:3-4 NAS). Children are not something we possess. We don't say, "This is mine." No, we are stewards of the children God gives us.

Are Your Kids Straight?

A child is not a sword in the hand of a warrior; a child is an arrow. There is a big difference between the two. An arrow in Palestine was made out of wood that was crooked. To get all of the bends and twists out, they supported it tightly in vices for several weeks. The wood was then sanded down and oiled before a sharp tip was mounted on it. Also, an arrow can go where you can't. That's why a child is an arrow. He or she is designed to go into the future where you cannot. As a good steward of the arrow, you must train, teach, and proclaim the Word of God in your house so your children can see it with their own eyes.

After you have cut, sanded, and polished the shaft and mounted the sharp tip of the arrow, then you must point it, by faith, toward the call God has placed on his or her life and release the arrow. Your task as a parent is to point your children toward that gift and call, and then release them to find their own identity in Christ. I like what was stated by one little girl. She said, "My name is Martha Bowers Taft. My great-grandfather was President of the United States. My grandfather was a U.S. senator. My daddy is an ambassador to Ireland, and I am a Brownie." She knew who she was.

When my son Isaac grew to be seven years old, we knew he had tremendous mental and athletic gifts, and we were grateful for them. But we also recognized that Isaac was still a seven-year-old boy. Isaac could mess up his daddy's hair once in a while, roll on the floor with him, and be a little boy. It is not wrong to be a little boy. Ronda didn't expect Isaac to act like he was 18 when he wasn't.

Dad, let your kids be kids. That may mean that you have to monitor some of the things you watch on TV. It may even require you to join in on some of those crazy games. Try it this week, even if you don't have any children. Just drag your old body out of the kitchen (maybe you've been eating too much anyhow), pull yourself away from the football game, and run around outside with the lightning bugs. When you catch one, don't squeeze it. Just watch that little glow, and something will happen inside.

Bless Your Children

Gary Smalley and John Trent tell this poignant story. Years ago a free-lance reporter from the *New York Times* who was interviewing Marilyn Monroe knew that in her early years, she had been passed around from orphan home to orphan home, or from foster parent to foster parent. This reporter asked Marilyn, "Did you ever feel loved by any of the foster families with whom you lived?" Marilyn said, "Yes. Once when I was seven or eight, the woman I was living with was putting on makeup, and I was watching her. And she was in a happy mood and she reached over and patted my cheeks with her rouge puff." And she said, "For that moment, I felt that she loved me." Marilyn Monroe had tears in her eyes, and they broke off the interview.

Why did Marilyn Monroe cry when she remembered this event? I believe that little orphan girl was looking for something vital, and in that little incident with the makeup, she received a portion of her dream. Like Marilyn Monroe, every human being longs for a blessing, a sign of approval—as proof that he or she is loved. For the love-parched little girl who later became Marilyn Monroe, that brief touch of tenderness from the woman in that foster home equalled buckets of love.

The Kiss of Life

God wants us as men to show affection for others, especially to our wives and children. The apostle Paul exhorted believers and church leaders, "Greet one another with a holy kiss" in Romans 16:16 and First Thessalonians 5:26. Instead, we often stop short because of society's sexual perversion and callousness. We think, "Well, maybe I should play it safe and avoid the embrace. A handshake will have to do."

Paul embraced Eutychus after he had fallen out of the window during a very long sermon. The Bible says Paul went down and embraced him and embraced the life of the Lord into his body (see Acts 20:10). Now I see more in this than just a resurrection. Many people have been healed and resurrected in their mental life simply by a timely embrace. It says, "In spite of any differences, arguments, or past failures, you are important and you are loved."

I have had real men, and I mean burly, strong men, come up and hug and kiss me on my cheek after an anointed conference. These men were not fruitcakes, they were simply responding to the Spirit of God that used me to tell them, "You are affirmed, you are approved, you are a man. God has granted you authority, and He blessed you in your manhood." These men could not help but respond to that.

Men have a bad habit of reserving embraces just for sexual intimacy, for times when we win something, and for tragic moments in our lives. We'll loosen up enough to hug somebody or receive a hug if we are standing or pacing in a hospital waiting room or at a funeral. Our deep need for physical closeness seems to become most apparent during times of catastrophe. When we see reports of an earthquake or a flood, or a severe accident on the news, we see men and women rush desperately to one another with open arms, clinging to each other. They just want the approval or security of another human being who cares.

They Did What?!

It's interesting that men who would never think of hugging or kissing another man will wildly pat another man's rump after winning a great athletic event! I can't believe the football players who run and hug each other, and kiss each other all over at the Superbowl. If anybody tried that any other time, they'd be spitting teeth all over the field. The typical modern, urban male has placed a spiritual and emotional armor around himself that says, "I don't want to touch because I've been hurt in the past."

Gary Smalley relates a true story about a Marine officer who had a deep desire to have his son, Brian, walk in his footsteps. He believed that discipline and backbone were of the utmost importance in the training of his son, so he decided, "I have to rule out tenderness, and affectionate behavior must be forbidden." He carefully chose all of Brian's athletic events and academic electives to groom him for a career as an officer. He only praised Brian when he scored a touchdown or earned high marks. Each time, however, this father immediately followed the praise with a lecture on how Brian could have done so much better.

Finally, Brian entered the Marine Corps just like his proud father. His father's joy was short-lived, however, because Brian seemed to be unable to take orders. His bad attitude led to a dishonorable discharge, and Brian's father said, "Brian, you're no longer welcome in our home. We don't want to see you anymore." Brian spent the next few years running from job to job. Despite his keen intelligence, he couldn't keep a job. He was engaged three times, but he broke off every engagement just before the wedding date. He was searching for approval.

Dad, Wake Up!

One night Brian received a call from his mother. "Brian, hurry and come home. Your father is dying of a heart attack." Throughout the flight, he kept repeating to himself, "I know Dad will listen. I just know our relationship can change. Tonight, I'm going to tell him and I'm going to receive something from my dad." He arrived at the hospital only to learn that his father had fallen into a coma. Brian waited for four hours, hoping his father would come out of the coma. When he died while still in the coma, the nurses on that shift said every corridor of the hospital echoed with young Brian's profuse cries: "Please Dad! Please Dad, please just tell me you love me, Dad! Tell me you love me! Wake up, Dad! Wake up."

Children desperately need their father's blessing. The Bible is filled with stories of this urgent search for paternal blessing. Nearly every child mentioned in the Bible received some kind of "laying on of hands." This is God's way for us to say, "You are accepted. Here is my love. Here is my blessing. Be encouraged, my child."

Jacob's deceptive theft of his older brother's paternal blessing led to a lifetime of heartache for Esau, who chose to value his appetite for food more than his inheritance from his father.

And it came to pass, as soon as Isaac had made an end of blessing Jacob, and Jacob was yet scarce gone out from the presence of Isaac his father, that Esau his brother came in from his hunting. ... And Isaac his father said unto him, Who art thou? And he said, I am thy son, thy firstborn Esau. And Isaac trembled very exceedingly, and said, Who?... And when Esau heard the words of his father, he cried with a great and exceeding bitter cry, and said unto his father, Bless me, even me also, O my father (Genesis 27:30,32-34).

We are still hearing that anguished cry, "Bless me, even me also, my father," but in our day satan is the thief. This painful cry has gone up for centuries, but it is especially loud in our society where millions of people are searching for a father's blessing. We have been taught that to really bless our children, we must make them happy. We naturally equate this false idea of happiness with buying them things. We never take the time to caress and hug them, or to bless them and pray over them.

Do It Like I Do It

We have missed the mark. Our children will not be ready to leave our home until they have received our parental approval and blessing. But thank God, a certain Jewish Rabbi took all the accumulated Scriptures of the Old Testament and embodied their truth in His person. He said, "Now I will come and demonstrate for you, above and beyond all of the bias and prejudice of the past, what God's heart is in old covenant practices of embracing, kissing, loving, hugging, and the laying on of hands. I'll bring you right into a new understanding of it."

Jesus did just that. Mark writes, "And they were bringing children to Him so that He might *touch them*..." (Mk. 10:13 NAS). After Jesus rebuked His disciples for hindering the children, then God the Son did something we need to carefully observe: "And He took them in His arms and began blessing them, laying His hands upon them" (Mk. 10:16 NAS).

Jesus touched, held, and embraced the little children. He was saying, "Look seminarians and future preachers, *this* is God, for God is love." In modern Orthodox Jewish homes, the father gives a weekly blessing to each of his children as part of a formal ceremony. Candles are lit and the time of blessing begins with the common elements of a shared meal, kissing, hugging, and the laying on of hands. As I researched this, I said, "God, this should be in the homes of Your New Covenant people."

Many of us just say, "Hey, bless you, son," but we don't take the time to have a real ceremony where we lay such a foundation of approval that our kids grow up knowing the love of God through the embraces and the warmth of Mom and Dad. When Isaac blessed Jacob, an embrace and a kiss were involved.

According to Smalley and Trent, Dr. Dolores Krieger, a professor of nursing at New York University, conducted research proving that there is a physiological benefit to touching one another. Hemoglobin is the pigment of the red blood cells that carry oxygen to our body tissues. Scientific studies have shown that when you lay hands on somebody, that person's hemoglobin levels instantly rise and oxygen is released in greater portions to the bloodstream. This was shown to help people recover from sickness quicker, and it immediately releases energy in the body.

UCLA Proves God's Point

Smalley and Trent also mention a UCLA study maintaining that for maximum emotional and physical health, you need from eight to ten "meaningful touches" a day.

Now apply this proposition to the Bible. Why is this such a loving book? It is filled with references to kisses, embraces, and laying on of hands. One of the first descriptions of believers under the New Covenant was that "...they shall lay hands on the sick, and they shall recover" (Mk. 16:18). Why? God knew that when He imparted part of His nature into our spirits, and we would touch somebody, God's Spirit would be released. The point is that He uses you and me to touch one another with His power.

What is a "meaningful touch"? It is "a gentle touch, a stroke, a hug given to or received from significant people." How much time do people spend stroking their cats and dogs, while their spouses and children are across the room literally starving for their touch and affection? Who is significant in your life? Hopefully that list includes your spouse, your children, your parents, your grandparents, your close friends, and the brothers and sisters in your church.

Smalley and Trent have found numerous studies that affirm the need for touch. A study conducted by Purdue University asked librarians to touch every other student over a specified period. As students were given their library cards during that period, one out of every two subjects received a touch from the librarians. Afterward, every student was interviewed. They didn't know ahead of time about the study, but every student who had been touched on the hand gave the researchers very favorable comments about the library and the librarian who touched them. This appreciation for touch is ingrained within us.

Another study found that the real motivation for prostitutes was not the desire for the sexual act, but a deep longing to be held and cuddled. I saw a picture of a prostitute in a publication matched with a story that put the person in a bad light. However, as I looked at the woman,

I thought, "You poor, tender thing." She looked like she was only about 19 years old, and through all the makeup I could see the hurt within her, the deep longing for approval. That doesn't excuse her sin, but it should make us aware that people we meet often come from painful backgrounds. If we found ourselves in their situation, perhaps we would have chosen a path of sin as well. That is why God warns us to be slow to judge others. Judgment starts in the household of God. He wants us to be a bridge to the world, to be a source of unconditional love and acceptance to a world starved for a father's blessing.

Hugs Are Not Fatal!

Dr. Ross Campbell said this: "In all my research and experience I have never known of one sexually disoriented person who had a warm, loving and affectionate father" (Smalley and Trent). Man of God, if you want your children to turn out right, then be a warm, loving, and affectionate father. There is something miraculous about touching and holding. At least twice a week before retiring, I used to get up in the night specifically to lay my hands on my son, Isaac, and quietly bless him in the name of Jesus. I've never heard of one report yet that claims too many hugs will kill you prematurely. It's just not there.

The problem with most of us is that we have never received the same unconditional approval from our parents that Jesus gave us through the cross. Years ago, before Ronda and I went to India as missionaries, I was very eager to get Dad and Grandpop to lay their hands on me. I wanted them to grant me the blessing of God. I never forgot that, for something is imparted through the laying on of hands.

Now if you are still hurting so bad that you can't bless your own children, God has a miracle in store for you.

Even if your father and grandfather are gone, you can still receive God's fatherly blessing today through the Holy Spirit. You need the touch of God's approval on your life. You may not be able to resurrect Mom or Dad, but you can know a father's love today because He has given you His Spirit, along with all things necessary for life and salvation (see 2 Pet. 1:3). He wouldn't leave you without a way of receiving this marvelous, divine approval.

It is important that we bless our children and one another. There's one problem with it, however: It's addictive. You'll want to continue to do it. Paul exhorted believers: "Greet all the brethren with an holy kiss" (1 Thess. 5:26; see also Rom. 16:16; 1 Cor. 16:20; 2 Cor. 13:12). Unfortunately, most of us refrain because we fear the society around us. We've been called to be the people of God, so rejoice and be exceedingly glad. Don't be offended when somebody wants to hug you or embrace you. Let people see the love of God manifested through you.

Chapter 9

Dare to Wear
Them Proudly

Real men love miracle turnarounds over impossible situations. They love to run to the rescue in times of trouble (but they hate to be the one who calls for help). Crisis situations bring people together. In times of war, men who never would have talked to one another otherwise are thrown together in foxholes, and for that season of crisis are dependent on one another for their very lives.

True manhood can only arise when a man knows who he is, where he is going, and why he is going there. Consider the Pioneer of manhood:

Jesus knowing that the Father had given all things into His hands, and that He was come from God, and went to God (John 13:3)

Jesus therefore, knowing all things that should come upon Him, went forth, and said unto them, Whom seek ye? (John 18:4).

*Looking unto Jesus the author and finisher of our faith;
who for the joy that was set before Him endured the cross,
despising the shame, and is set down at the right hand of
the throne of God* (Hebrews 12:2).

Because Jesus knew who He was, where He was going,
and why He had been sent by the Father, the living
Church of Jesus Christ is full of God and holds a healing
message for all men in times of crisis. Real men who know
who they are and whom they serve inspire other men.
They move nations and command authority as God gives
them grace. Every man goes through a time of training
and testing, followed by an "initiation" or blessing from
God that confirms the longing in his heart and releases
him to fulfill the call of God on his life. Unfortunately, too
many of us quit too soon. We doubt our identity and stop
the process in the middle of the stream, or we allow others to stop it.

We Need a "Boxer Rebellion"

*Then Jesus arrived from Galilee at the Jordan coming to
John, to be baptized by him. But John tried to prevent
Him, saying, "I have need to be baptized by You, and do
You come to me?" But Jesus answering said to him, "Per-
mit it at this time; for in this way it is fitting for us to ful-
fill all righteousness." Then he permitted Him. And after
being baptized, Jesus went up immediately from the
water; and behold the heavens were opened, and He saw
the Spirit of God descending as a dove, and coming upon
Him, and behold, a voice out of the heavens, saying,
"This is My beloved Son, in whom I am well-pleased"*
(Matthew 3:13-17 NAS).

Jesus said, "...there is not a greater prophet than John
the Baptist..." (Lk. 7:28). Just before he was martyred, as
he sat in the blackness of a dungeon, John began to doubt
what he has seen. This is the same man who declared to
his disciples, "...He who sent me to baptize in water said

to me, 'He upon whom you see the Spirit descending and remaining upon Him, this is the one who baptizes in the Holy Spirit.' And I have seen, and have borne witness that this is the Son of God" (Jn. 1:33-34 NAS).

In the end, John was reassured by the words of Jesus and gave his life because he dared to stand like a man and declare the truth of God to a king in sin. Our generation is filled with millions of people who are bound and looking for a way out of their pain. These are times of crisis. These are the times when men of God are needed, men who dare to stand up and wear their boxer shorts proudly! We need them to stand before scoffing bureaucrats, fearful leaders, and hurting families and clearly declare: "Behold, the Lamb of God who takes away the sin of the world! ... Behold, the Man!" (Jn. 1:29b,19:5b)

When Jesus stood in the chilly waters of the Jordan River, He was in a place of transition. The transition began in the wilderness with fasting, prayer, and fierce temptation designed by satan to cast doubt upon and cloud the purpose of the Messiah's calling. Jesus had lived a little over 30 years in Joseph and Mary's house, growing up in obedience to His earthly father and in submission to the greater will of His heavenly Father. Like Jesus, you and I may also find ourselves standing in the middle of a muddy river facing catastrophic change and a new direction for our lives.

The chilly waters of the Jordan River empty into the Dead Sea, an inland sea with no outlet that was known as a place of death and filth. Naaman didn't even want to go into the Jordan, it was so dirty, yet Jesus, the Son of God, was literally launched into public ministry as He stood in that dirty, muddy water. The truth is that He went in to pull us out of our muddy messes.

Caught in the Creek

Now we find ourselves standing in the muddy waters of transition. Don't think this is the work of the devil—God's hand is upon you for good and not for evil. It is time for you to "wear your boxer shorts proudly" in His strength because it is time for you to help other men "come of age" in their faith and manhood!

Let's go down to the Jordan with Jesus. Let's come up out of that water immediately and enter the new life of Jesus Christ. Just as that victory yanked Jesus right out of the grave, it will yank you right out of your grave today! It is so powerful that it will continue to deliver everyone you lead to the water in His name! When the power of God is on the scene, you just don't need to be concerned about your own strengths and weaknesses, or about the opinions of others. The only opinion that counts is the opinion of the One who made you.

Okay, so nobody understands you or believes that you have heard from God. Can you imagine what Jesus, the Son of God, went through? Imagine a scene at the synagogue three years before Jesus stood in the muddy Jordan. He is a 27-year-old man walking to the local synagogue when everybody runs past Him to see "Rabbi Ben Blessing," bumping and shoving past Him in the process. All the while, nobody even recognizes that Jesus, the very Son of God, is beside them. Have you ever known that you had the anointing? Have you ever had God speak to you about something He was going to accomplish through your life—but it has not yet come to pass? Everybody seems to be running by you or bumping into you to get to somebody else.

Listen, man of God: There came a day in Jesus' life when He was catapulted by the hand of God from obscurity to renown in a flash! Suddenly everybody knew that Jesus was the Anointed of God, for the heavens opened up! Once God releases you for a specific purpose, then He supplies the anointing needed to accomplish the supernatural task. Once the Holy Spirit descended on Jesus, there was no need to call for John the Baptist

anymore. Jesus had been appointed. It was His time. You
are also anointed, and there is a day for your appointment. When the manifestation of what you have been
promised comes to pass, you will pass from obscurity to
renown according to God's plan.

Here Are the Keys, Son

Whether you are called to preach from a pulpit, or
minister in the shadows behind prison bars, or lovingly
disciple young hearts in a Sunday school classroom behind the sanctuary, your time will come. What a day that
will be! You have stood on the promises of God, and you
have confessed His Word with your mouth. Many nights
you have secretly soiled your pillow with tears, but you
said, "God, I trust in You. I don't look to man because I
know You are truthful; Your Word shall come to pass."
The day will come when God will give you the "keys to the
car," and the manifestation that you have been waiting for
will begin to happen in your life. That is the time to cele-
brate! God has spoken: "You might have thought you
were anointed, you may have doubted your anointing, but
I tell you, your day of appointment has come!"

We often feel like we're standing under a "closed"
heaven. Most of us have to admit that we've prayed,
"God, I know You're real, but I don't understand why I
don't have the answers." We also have to admit that we've
tried to do things out of our own strength out of impa-
tience, long before the total inheritance and anointing
have come. All of this will come on the day of its appointment. God has been with us all along, but He moves in
phases in our lives. We have a "progressive" walk with
Him, which means we're growing in our wisdom, understanding, and patience.

Man of God, when you finally get tired enough to lay your worries down on the rock like Jacob did, then you will begin to have dreams and revelations. You will have divine visitations and discover that God had you in His heart and hand all along!

Jesus saw Nathanael coming to Him, and saith of him, Behold an Israelite indeed, in whom is no guile! Nathanael saith unto Him, Whence knowest Thou me? Jesus answered and said unto him, Before that Philip called thee, when thou wast under the fig tree, I saw thee. Nathanael answered and saith unto Him, Rabbi, Thou art the Son of God; Thou art the King of Israel. Jesus answered and said unto him, Because I said unto thee, I saw thee under the fig tree, believest thou? thou shalt see greater things than these (John 1:47-50).

Jehovah Shama, the God we serve, is here. When the heavens open up and you see the preexistence of God, then you begin to understand why certain things happen and why there are "delays of God" in your life. God has been there all along. You may not have seen it with your physical eye, but you don't know how precious you are to God. We are sitting beside Jesus. Jesus is with us. I love it when the Holy Spirit comes on people and they begin to realize that they have a personal walk with Jesus Christ.

We have to go through transition in order to get to the place where the heavens open. It may be time for the heavens to open for you. If this is so, then you are about to see the throne and the authority of God as you have never seen it before. You are about to enter a blessing in your life that you never thought possible for you. Jesus has come to tell you, "I saw you when you didn't even know I was looking at you. I was sitting beside you when you thought you were too far away from Me in your own sin. I was there because you are Mine."

God Knows Your Feet Are Wet

He was always there in the past, and He is with you even now. His Spirit can penetrate even the thickest walls to bring joy in the morning. When you don't think you are going to make it, He gets through for you. When you felt like quitting your job, and when your marriage was falling apart, you managed to worship Him anyway and He invaded your job site and intervened in your marriage to pull it all back together. You may feel like you are losing your son and daughter right now to drugs or to the things of the world, but look up. Your feet may be buried in the muddy waters of trial and transition, but the Holy Spirit is descending even now on you. You are the man God has chosen, and His anointing is about to rise up within you.

I tell you, a fresh anointing is on its way. He is raising up a generation of *real men* who find their strength in something more powerful than muscles or macho attitudes. You are one of the chosen men who are destined to step into the Jordan for a death to self so you can emerge from the muddy waters with God's anointing to serve others. The miracle will begin in your home, in your marriage, and in your children. Then it will spread to every life you come into contact with! Our victory as men is rooted in Jesus the Christ, the Anointed One.

It is time to wear your godly manhood proudly. Why don't you go into work a little early tomorrow morning. Instead of murmuring and complaining, get there before everybody else and anoint the place in the name of Jesus Christ! Do some commando work and confound the enemy behind the lines. If you have an elevator, go up and down that shaft proclaiming the Word of God in Jesus' name. Boldly declare that the Kingdom of God is coming to that office. Declare as a soldier of occupation that you are not going to allow the enemy to rule and harass those who work with you any longer. Realize that Jesus Christ is there because His anointing dwells in you!

Your Name Is...

Pray for your family every morning and night. Bless your father and mother if they are still alive. Bless your wife and children, naming them one by one, and declare God's Word over them. We're living in a generation that has lost fatherhood. Since we get our identity from our fathers, it is time for God's chosen fathers to rise up and give godly identity to their children and spiritual offspring!

Rachel, the beloved wife of Jacob, died in childbirth. Now Jacob, (deceiver) whose name had been changed to Israel by this point, had a background of low self-esteem. He had been given an evil name at birth, and it took the intervention of God to change his name and his life. When Jacob entered the tent at the end of the labor, he discovered that his dear wife had died. As Rachel was suffering in childbirth, she uttered the name, *Benoni*, which means "child of my sorrows." Can you imagine going through your life with the burden of that name: "Child of Mama's sorrows"?

When Jacob came in, he entered as a man who knew what it was to have a curse broken over his life. God had given him the new name of *Israel*, or "Prince." While he looked down at the limp body of Rachel, the nurse told him his son had been named "Child of my sorrows" by his wife. Jacob immediately recoiled, and he exercised the right and authority of a father to name his children. Jacob told the nurse, "That child shall not be called 'child of sorrows.' His name shall be 'Benjamin.' He shall be called 'child of my strength,' and the 'child of my right hand,' the 'child of my blessing.' His name is Benjamin, for he is going to be the strength of my right hand, and kings shall

come through the tribe of Benjamin!" (my paraphrase of
Genesis 35:18).

More Than a Male

We have produced a generation of men who cannot
find their fathers, of men who are male enough to sire a
child, but not man enough to raise a child. Their absentee
fathers, alcoholic fathers, workaholic fathers, and preaching fathers were all so distracted with "busyness" that they
never took the time to tell the men of this new generation
who they are. That fact is, that to a great extent, you are
who your father says you are! Without direction from
Dad, that boy, that teenager, that young man will go
through life spinning out of control, joining cliques and
gangs, and going from this perversion to that perversion
in a wandering search for his name. Many women are
married to nameless men who don't know who they are.
They often beat their wives in anger, and unfaithfully go
from bed to bed, even though they can't be truly intimate.
They are unable to open up emotionally, and they're uncomfortable with intimacy. Why? These men have never
had an affectionate father tell them who they are. They
are uncomfortable with intimacy because they have been
raised as nameless babies.

We can't go out and transform the world unless we
first move into our own identity. You can't give somebody
what you don't have. Even Jesus could not begin His ministry until His Father told Him who He was. Every son will
tell you that they perform better when Dad is there. I
thought maybe I would make Isaac too tense by being at
one of his sporting events, but he always says, "Dad, I want
you there! I want you there on time." Why? My son wants
my approval, whether he is driving for a basket, trying to
throw a fastball for a strike, or attempting to score a goal
as center striker on his soccer team. He's looking for approval, so I give it to him! "Go ahead son! Go for it. Go for

the score. Go ahead and strike him out. Drive for that basket, son, and get that basket because you're Dad's son!" Sons need to hear who they are.

If you go down to the chilly waters of the Jordan, your place of transition, you will begin to look up and you will start to see the heavens open for you. And God Himself will declare who you are. You are not what life has dealt you. You are not who they said you are. You are not what your situation has said. You are not what your circumstances have been crying out to you. Allow God to lay His hands on you. Allow God to speak to you and tell you who you are.

Then reclaim all of your masculine rights and privileges. Dare to worship God with zeal and excitement in the pattern established by David the warrior, king, and prophet. Dare to tenderly nurture your children and love your wife by laying down your life for her. Dare to stand in the day of trouble secure in your God and your anointing to shield and protect. Dare to be a man in the name of the Man named Jesus!

As men we need to praise God until our childhood fear is broken. We need to praise Him until we get our strength back. We need to worship the Lord in the chilly waters of the Jordan until the heavens open up and we hear our Father declare exactly who we are:

> "You are My chosen one. You're not going to be the son of My sorrows; you are going to be the son of My strength and the son of My blessing!"

In the Spirit, this is Father's Day. This is the day of deliverance for dads. It is time to rise from our knees and anoint our loved ones and our possessions in Jesus' name. Our children will not have to go through what we've gone through because the King resides in us.

Chapter 10

Words From Real Men

Godly men of national prominence are an invaluable resource to the Kingdom of God. My good friends Gary Carter and scout Jack Hawkins have arranged TV interviews for me with several *real men* of God who are also some of the major league's top professional baseball players, managers, and future hall of famers. Here is what some of them had to say about manhood, fatherhood, the Christian walk, and life in the national spotlight.

Gary Carter at Veterans Stadium

Pastor Dewey: During the last 15 years, Gary Carter has been the premier catcher in major league baseball. Welcome Gary.

Gary Carter: I really believe that the Holy Spirit is moving through professional sports. It is important for role models to stand up for Jesus. I have always stood for Jesus, and I know a lot of players who are coming out and expressing themselves as well.

We have a Baseball Chapel program every Sunday for guys who can't really get to a church on a Sunday morning. We play games every day, and we usually have Sunday afternoon games that force us to leave our hotel by bus by 9:30 or 10:00 in the morning. The Baseball Chapel gives us all the opportunity to worship together and to have a fellowship as a team. It's a real good opportunity, and I think it brings a ball club closer together.

Even before the days of the Baseball Chapel, especially in New York, we started putting together Bible studies. Scott Oplinger, who is with "Athletes In Action," used to come out to my house, and we would invite players and their wives to join us for Bible study. We would get into the Word for about an hour-and-a-half, and then we'd throw some burgers on the grill for a really nice time of fellowship.

It's important to know what Jesus has done for us, and that He died for our sins. I don't know where my career would have been if I didn't know Him as Lord and Savior. I give Him all the glory and praise. I really believe that all my success has come from Him. If people understood the importance of what Jesus stands for, their lives could be better as well.

Pastor Dewey: You've known adversity of course. Your mom died from leukemia when you were 12 years old, and you've had other personal tragedies in your life. Some people claim that Christianity is just a crutch. What would you say about facing life's situations on your own, as opposed to knowing that you have a personal relationship with Jesus?

Gary: The greatest thing about knowing Jesus as your Lord and Savior is knowing that even if you're alone somewhere without a friend to talk to, no matter what situation you may be in, He is always there. He is always ready to listen, help, and direct you.

Prayer is powerful. I've seen miracles happen through the prayers of my wife's Bible study class in Florida. When emergencies arise, they get everybody on the phone and get a prayer chain going. I'm telling you, Dewey, it is unbelievable! Those people even prayed for my knee the time Dr. Andrews performed the surgery on it. He said my recovery was going to take about a year. But I worked hard and prayed, "Lord, if it is not meant for me to continue to play, so be it. But if I am to play, then instill in me the power to go and work out and get myself into the best of shape. Allow me the opportunity to play again."

Once I got into my workout sessions, my knee started feeling better, but I still had no team since I had left the New York Mets. The next prayer was to go to a team that had a lot of Christians. It was a miracle that I ended up with the Giants for a year after my recovery, since that San Francisco club has a good base of solid Christian guys with great foundations. More than half of the players are Christians! There are always going to be temptations in baseball, though. It is just a matter of trying to overcome those. I feel that I'm better off by far because I spend my spare time on the road just fellowshiping with my teammates and learning more about God's Word. That's the one thing I think that was missing throughout most of my career.

On most of the major league teams I played with, the guys would look at me and think, *This guy's too good to be true! He loves his wife, he loves his family, and he doesn't go out and fool around!* This is what the Lord wanted me to do, so I did it with His grace. Of course I was criticized and looked down upon, and there was a lot of jealousy, maybe because I had my life together. I knew what I wanted to provide for my family *after* baseball. The Holy Spirit is powerful, and He moves in response to prayer. The Book of James talks about the trials and tribulations we all go through. If it was just wine and roses, life would be too easy in this world. We all have to go through some adversity at one time or another.

My mother's death was a very devastating blow when I was 12 years old. But I know that God wanted me to live my life in this fashion and to be a role model that is willing to stand for Him. Even in the adversity, the loss of a loved one, and all the injuries and things that I've gone through in my professional baseball career, I've had my eyes focused on Jesus. He is the One who has brought me through everything.

Pastor Dewey: Do you believe that the adversity gave you a drive that you would not have experienced if it had not been for the tragedy?

Gary: Well, when I returned from my mother's funeral, I came back home and threw a no-hitter in the first game that I pitched! That game was for Mom. At that time, sports were the most prominent thing in my life, although we were always a church-going family. It wasn't until I signed a professional contract and had the opportunity of rooming with John Boccabella that I knew what Christ was all about. When I finally accepted Jesus Christ as Lord during that spring training camp in March of 1973, I felt it really turned my life around. I felt that inner peace and joy. A lot of people who came to see me said they noticed that my smile seemed to radiate something. It's pretty simple: it was Jesus.

Pastor Dewey: How do you get along with other guys on the team who say, "What goes, Carter? Are you some 'Goody Two Shoes'? I mean, what's the deal? Let's go out and drink; let's get the women and have a big time!" How do you handle that kind of pressure?

Gary: The lie says that a real man doesn't attend church because he doesn't need anybody. Yet, it seems like a number of the heroes today are saying, "We do need people. We do need Christ. We need the Church and one another." Nobody is an island. I know that when I first started out I made mistakes and things as well, but I still had my focus on Jesus.

Dewey, to know Jesus Christ on a personal level is the greatest commitment you can make. It was the greatest decision in my life! My marriage comes right behind my confession of faith, but my commitment to Christ was greater to me than the Hall of Fame, home runs, top RBIs, averages, MVP awards, and game-winning hits in the world series.

We all are destined for certain things in this life. I think we are all put on this earth for a purpose. Whether it is to glorify God, or whether it is to be a professional baseball player, or a pastor, or whatever it may be, I think we are all here for a reason. And if you understand that reason and become the child of God to live for Him and by Him, you can't go wrong.

Pastor Dewey: You changed uniforms again.

Gary: That was really like a dream come true, Dewey. I played 12 years in Montreal, 5 years with the Mets, and 1 year in San Francisco. Now I'm back home where it all began. I followed the Dodgers when I was a kid and grew up in the Fullerton area. It's where we are living right now. It's really special because I've been able to spend some real quality time with my family as well.

Pastor Dewey: Gary, what advice do you have for young guys wanting to make it in sports?

Gary: I think the biggest thing is to be disciplined and to apply yourself by always giving it your very best. If you can look in the mirror and say on any given day, "I gave it my very best," then that is all you can ask of yourself. For Little Leaguers growing up, I think the important thing to keep in mind is to go out and enjoy the game. Don't make it a profession at that early age. Above all, get to know Jesus Christ on a personal basis.

Orel Herchesier

Pastor Dewey: Orel, tell us about how you met Jesus Christ.

Orel Herchesier: Well, in 1979, I became a professional baseball player, and I met a baseball player who was a

Christian. I thought I was already a Christian at the time just because I was born in America and went to church on Easter and Christmas! Besides that, my parents told me that I was a Christian. This player, Butch Wickenshier, got me intrigued about reading the Bible that was always in the bottom drawer of my dresser. I came to the realization that I was a sinner, so one day in the little Buckaroo Hotel in Arizona, I knelt down next to my bed and asked the Lord into my life. There were no bangs, whistles, fireworks, or big explosions, but at that moment I felt peace, and I knew that the future was taken care of.

Before I was a Christian, I used to get real frustrated and jealous of other players who got the headlines or moved forward ahead of me to the big leagues. Once I became a Christian, I realized that there was a bigger plan. God just wanted me to give my best with the ability He gave me. Then I was responsible to tell people where the ability came from. Having Christ in my life and knowing He has a plan for me makes it easier for me to face daily problems and challenges.

Pastor Dewey: Orel, there is a real sense of restoration and revival in the nation, but at the same time, there is a deterioration of family life.

Orel: Families need to spend time together and love one another. There is an emptiness for love in the world right now, so we need to make sure our homes are as full of love as possible. Kids need to know there's warmth at home, and a place to come where they can be secure.

Veteran All-Star center fielder Brett Butler was on hand, so here is what he had to say:

Brett Butler

Pastor Dewey: Brett, what happened in your life? I understand you've been a Christian for awhile. How did you meet Jesus?

Brett Butler: In 1973, I went to a Fellowship of Christian Athletes conference in Fort Collins, Colorado. A man asked me, "Brett, if you were to die tonight, would you go to Heaven?" I just didn't have that assurance, so later, when I was by myself in my room, I got on my knees and asked Christ into my life. I was just a sophomore in high school. From that time on I decided to try to live a holy life—but I tried to do it on my own. I conveniently put God in my back pocket. My god was baseball, and I worshiped my dream to be a major league baseball player. I was drafted in June of 1979 and started going through the minor leagues. Finally, I was invited to big league camp. I can see how God directed my life. At one point, I was guilt-ridden over the fact that women were a problem in my life. I got on my knees and confessed it to God. That spring, I was the last person cut in big league camp and I ended up in triple A, and I was a little disappointed. Then I went down to Richmond and met a woman named Evelyn Ballach. On our third date, I sat her on the couch and said, "You are going to think I'm the craziest fool in the world, but I believe God put you in my life." God works miracles. After the third date, we knew we were going to get married.

God has directed my steps throughout the course of my career in the major leagues, and He has helped me cope with the problems of wealth and fame and the crazy things that have happened in baseball. God still corrects me as a Father corrects a son.

Pastor Dewey: Brett, one theme has come through all the ballplayers we talked to today: God has a plan for your life and He has divine appointments for you. He has arranged appointments that lead you into a deeper walk, and confirm you as a son of God.

Brett: I think that a lot of people think God is a good luck charm. That is not the fact. I have four children whom I love dearly. But if my children do something wrong, I have to correct them for their own good. God is doing this for me. People chase after the money and fame, thinking that will make them happy. They don't realize that God made us all with one spot in our heart that is reserved for God. He is the only one who can fill it.

Bob Boone

Pastor Dewey: Bob, you have been the "Van Gogh" of catchers in major league baseball. Your career has spanned 19 years, and you were an All-Star. You were also a Golden Glove winner seven times! You played with the Philadelphia Phillies and California Angels, and you finished your last two years as a player with the Kansas City Royals. What is going on in your life?

Bob Boone: I've been named the manager of the Kansas City Royals, and I'm very excited about the position, even though I felt kind of down about the contract dispute that put the game on hold. I've given the situation to the Lord, and He has never failed me yet. I played until I was 43 years old, which is somewhat ridiculous actually. I trained diligently for 15 years in a year-round program, and I went through four knee surgeries. Many prayers have been said for me, and I asked God a lot of times to help heal me. That allowed me to get through things.

One of the things that God gave me was a passion for baseball. God gave me a gift of being able to catch and throw a baseball and hit a little bit. He kind of shorted me on the running speed, and I was a little upset with Him there. But I found that the game so intrigued me that the more I learned, the more I realized I didn't know.

I really believe that one of the things that allowed me to compete until I was 43 years old was that burning desire to play the game. I refused to give in to the age factor. I can remember leaving spring training after I had been essentially fired or didn't make the team thinking, *This is it*. I was driving across the desert from Phoenix back to my home in Anaheim, California. There was a peace about me when it was finally time to leave the field and move into management.

Pastor Dewey: Was there a certain point when Christ became a living reality?

Bob: I can't say I was really a Christian as a boy. I was a good boy and a good student who did the right things and got to the major leagues without ever really knowing Christ. When I got into baseball around 1975, I met a fellow named Watson who approached me. He was a retired writer out of Detroit who knew my dad. He was starting something called the Baseball Chapel program. He wanted me to be a leader. I tried everything to get out of it, but I couldn't think fast enough. So I became the leader. We had fascinating speakers come into the clubhouse to speak, and it was my job to coordinate getting the players to the meeting. We met in everything from laundry rooms to shower bays. In the early days there was Gary Maddox, Mike Schmidt, and myself. In those days, if you read the Bible or were a Christian, somehow you were a sissy, so most guys were leery of coming in. I started getting introduced to God's Word and to what God's plan was, and it started weighing on my heart. My wife was in there and she had been raised in a Baptist family background, but really she wasn't a Christian because she didn't know what that meant.

Sue and I started getting into the Word together, and we were blessed with a great man named Wendall Campton, who was just probably the most brilliant Bible scholar

I've ever been around. In the off season in 1978, I finally accepted Christ into my heart. Everything was going perfect. I had three lovely kids, a great wife, money, fame, a business interest. However, I still found that there was an emptiness that Jesus filled. When I started on this path I hadn't even known there was a void.

Pastor Dewey: You don't have to be a wimp to follow Christ.

Bob: That's the message I preach, especially to kids. That's going to be my first message as manager of the Royals in spring training. The Kansas City Royals are going to be or a team headed by Bob Boone, and that bunch is going to be a team of warriors. There is a biblical base to it. I expect every player to give his best at all times—that's what a warrior does. That is our personal contract with God. God will supply our needs, but we must give God everything. God gave me an ability to block home plate, so the job God assigned me as a player was not to let an opposing player touch home plate. I certainly wasn't going to hurt anybody, but nobody was going to touch that plate either! (It got a little hard when Bo Jackson was bearing down on me, but that was my job.)

Pastor Dewey: Do you have any final remarks for children and fathers?

Bob: Give it everything you have and play it for the fun. Win, lose, or draw, give your heart to what you do. It may make losing an emotional experience, but the fact is, there is still tomorrow.

Works Cited

Cole, Edwin Louis. *Maximized Manhood* (Whitaker House, 1982), pp. 144-147.

Dalbey, Gordon. *Healing the Masculine Soul* (Word Publishing, 1988), pp. 43, 117-129, 174-184.

Duff, Karl. *Restoration of Men* (Destiny Image, 1990), pp. 1-54.

Gilder, George. *Wealth and Poverty* (Basic Books, 1981).

Hardenbrook, Weldon M. *Missing From Action* (Thomas Nelson, 1987), pp. 10, 86-87, 95-100, 118-134, 167-176.

Hybels, Bill. *Christians in a Sex Crazed Culture* (Victor Books, 1989), pp. 45-75.

———. *Laws That Liberate* (Victor Books, 1985), pp. 79-91.

Jakes, Bishop T.D. Manpower tape series, 1994.

LeSourd, Leonard E. *Strong Men Weak Men* (Chosen Books, 1990), pp. 245-248.

McDowell, Josh. *How to Help Your Child Say No* (Word Books, 1987), pp. 125-132.

McDowell, Josh and Dick Day. *Why Wait?* (Here's Life Publishers, 1987), pp. 264-267.

Mossholder, Ray. *Marriage Plus* (Creation House, 1990), pp. 60-70, 126, 190, 211.

Moyers, Bill. *A World of Ideas*, Vol. II (Doubleday, 1990), pp. 267-284.

Paulk, Earl. *Sex Is God's Idea* (K Dimension Publishers, 1985).

Smalley, Gary and John Trent. *The Blessing* (Pocket Books, 1986), pp. 44-49.

Thompson, Steve. Confronting the Spirit of Jezebel tape, 1994.

Wright, Donald. *Tonight, We Wrestle* (Treasure House, 1994), pp. 102-109, 118-120, 139-143.

Additional Life-changing teaching material from the ministry of
Pastor Dewey Friedel.

"... for the earth will be full of the knowledge of the Lord, as the waters cover the sea."

Breakthrough Series - (Prices include postage and handling)

Healing The Masculine Soul (6 tapes) - $26.95
The Radical Preacher (4 tapes) - $19.95
Blessings and Curses (3 tapes) - $14.95
Dianoia, Releasing The Creative Side Of Your Mind (3 tapes) - $14.95
Miracle Stoppers (3 tapes) - $14.95
Biblical Meditation (3 tapes) - $14.95
Who's right? - Controversy Over The Faith Movement (3 tapes)- $14.95
No Monkey Business - Creation vs. Evolution (3 tapes) - $14.95
Honor Between Spouses (3 tapes) - $14.95
God's Transformational Church (2 tapes) - $9.95
Man and Woman (5 tapes) - $24.95
The Real Faith - A Breakthrough Understanding Of The Book Of
Revelation (3 parts, 9 tapes) - $44.95
Releasing Angel Power (3 tapes) - $14.95
So Long Wilderness (4 tapes) - $19.95
Thinking Increase (13 tapes) - $64.95
Developing Mental Toughness (4 tapes) - $19.95
Eagle Christians (2 tapes) - $9.95
Praise Is Worship! (4 tapes) - $19.95
Spit Or Anointing? (2 tapes) - $9.95
What Time Is It? (3 part series, 9 tapes total) - $44.95
Renewing The Mind, Developing A Prosperous Soul (7 tapes) - $34.95
Does Jesus Still Appear? - Full Disclosure (2 tapes) - $9.95

SINGLE TAPES

The Force of Favor
A Look At Heaven And Hell
Jezebel , It Is Mountain Moving Time
Victoria's Secret Is Out - Women's Meeting
Buckle Up, How To Live And Not Die
Sheba Is Coming, The Laugh Of Faith
The Salt Covenant, Activating Angels
See It Before You Receive It
Black Is Beautiful - The Cushites Are Coming
You Can Be Like Jabez - Better Than Average
Overcoming Racism

Videos

Wrestling On The Rock - Pastor Dewey wrestles Bam Bam Bigelow.
Great testimonies for your children.
3 Great Questions American's Are Asking: (see one of the greatest
healings of the last 2 decades)

Baseball Videos- Pastor Dewey interviews all-star baseball players as
they speak out about Jesus, fatherhood, and developing a winner's
attitude. (call for more information)

Ordering Information - Call for a free comprehensive tape catalog.
Single tapes are $5.00 -Videos are $19.95 each.
Prices include postage and handling.
Call 1-800-570-1265 to order or write: Shore Christian Center, P.O.
Box 515, Allenwood, NJ 08720
We accept MC, Visa, Amex, and Discover.